LOVE HIM MADLY

LOVE HIM MADLY

An Intimate Memoir of Jim Morrison

Judy Huddleston

CHICAGO
REVIEW
PRESS

An A Cappella Book

First edition
Published by Chicago Review Press, Incorporated
814 North Franklin Street
Chicago, Illinois 60610

ISBN 978-1-61374-750-6

Sections of this book were previously published in a different form as *This Is the End, My Only Friend*.

Cover design: Rebecca Lown
Cover photographs: Jim Morrison, 1970 (Michael Ochs Archives/Getty Images); (*inset*) the author, 1970 (courtesy Judy Huddleston)
Interior design: PerfecType, Nashville, TN

Library of Congress Cataloging-in-Publication Data
Huddleston, Judy.
    Love him madly : an intimate memoir of Jim Morrison / Judy Huddleston.
— First edition.
        p. cm.
    "Sections of this book were previously published in a different form as This is the end— my only friend"—Title page verso.
    ISBN 978-1-61374-750-6 (pbk.)
    1. Morrison, Jim, 1943–1971. 2. Rock musicians—United States—Biography.
    I. Huddleston, Judy. This is the end—my only friend. II. Title.
    ML420.M62H83 2013
    782.42166092—dc23
    [B]
                                        2012048500

Printed in the United States of America
5 4 3 2 1

Contents

Foreword

I see you've got your mitts on *Love Him Madly*. You must be a Doors fan. So am I. Fascinated with Jim Morrison? So am I.

Buckle yourself in for a dizzying ride, dear reader.

C'mon, just let yourself go; fall into the hazy, trippy, incense-scented past; slide into a young girl's budding fascination and ultimate romance with the Lizard King and his obvious attraction to her innocence and tortured devotion. Sometimes Judy Huddleston loved Jim Morrison desperately; other times she swore to stay away from his unpredictable rages, middle-of-the-night phone calls, and long disappearances. He confounded her, pissed her off, and shattered her heart more than once. But she never turned him away, sometimes sought him out—and who can blame her? Yes, he could be eerily menacing, but Jim could also be a precocious tease, inviting Judy into his tumultuous private thoughts and under the covers of his very messy bed.

By revealing her long-term, on-and-off love affair with Jim Morrison, Judy Huddleston has somehow been able to demythologize an eternal rock god, shedding light on this revered creature without defaming, denouncing, or damaging his escalating myth or his deepening mystery.

Reading this potently felt account of her long-term love affair with a youthful up-and-comer turned local celebrity, rock god, Sunset Strip fixture, worldwide phenomenon, dangerous felon, down-and-out drunkard, and audacious Paris-bound poet took me back to my own heady, madcap days during Hollywood's rock-and-roll heyday. I knew Jim, and I watched with curiosity, amazement, horror, sorrow, and hope as he pitched himself headfirst into audiences, gutters, and headlines, careening onto the music charts and into trouble all over the world.

Teenage Judy was there for him when his romance with Pam Courson turned into another screaming nightmare and he found himself teetering on the streets, on the prowl again. Luckily Judy kept diaries chronicling her many liaisons with Jim, and she enthralls us with their conversations held in the dark of night, in the heat of passion—conversations about life and death, love and angst, freedom, sex, monogamy, religion and spirituality, the here and now, and what might be waiting for us on the other side. Gazing so longingly and deeply into Jim's eyes drove Judy mad.

If you've never been high before (and even if you have), this book will get you there.

—Pamela Des Barres

When I was seventeen, I fell in love with a singer. At the end of a dilapidated green pier in Venice, in a club renovated with fake cheetah skins, the spotlight shone through dark blue silence and caught him at the microphone. He paused inside the softly lit circle; pale light played over his face and held it; a new kingdom had begun. He had pale skin—a fine, white translucency. He had delicate molding—the precision of his hip bones. He had dark hair—near black, lustrous. His beauty was injured, unyielding, artless. Jim took in the audience and closed his eyes; his delicate, destructible features drew an involuntary sigh from the crowd, a breath he gathered into himself. Transformed, he opened his eyes and began to sing. His deep baritone projected a presence I'd once known but had forgotten until that hypnotic moment. As in a polite introduction to the occult, no drawbacks were mentioned. . . .

I spent the first eleven months of that year trekking across cities, a bacchante following her ancient god. I left my boyfriend, the human race, and reality—there was only Jim.

Trouble Child

I dentifying marks?" the nurse asked.

"What?"

"Do you have any identifying marks?'

"Oh . . ." I touched my face. "These indentations here, by my nose—from chicken pox. And this shiny spot on my forehead from a rock."

"Don't you have any birthmarks, any scars?" Her full lips pursed in and down.

"I have this." I held up my wrist. The meticulous series of crosshatches formed a maroon Y over blue veins. The nurse smiled sympathetically and wrote, "Distinguished by light freckles, hair worn in bangs." I put my arm back on the table and looked away.

"The doctor said you were pretty," she said, glancing across the admitting room toward the former hippie who had interviewed me earlier. We'd been at the same love-ins at Elysian Park.

"Really? Can I see?" Smiling, the nurse nodded and pushed the paper toward me in a conspiratorial gesture. "Oh, he did. That was nice." I shrugged.

"Don't you think you're pretty?" she probed.

"I used to be . . . when I was young, I guess."

"It says here you're in your twenties."

"I know."

"That's young."

"Not for me," I said, beginning to regret acting civil and sane. I had, after all, just been admitted to a mental hospital. I glanced at the skinny red second hand of the institutional clock. The plastic dome covering the black numbered hours was no longer transparent but chipped, scarred, and grayed with age. I looked down at my wrists and neatly typed plastic bracelet stating my new identity. It was 1975; I'd just become an inmate of Ward 4-A.

The soft rubber soles of the nurse's shoes made sure, gliding contact with the worn linoleum floor; the squeaky noise echoed down the still corridor. We walked past rows of rooms—some open, some shut, each with a sliding window encased in the upper third of the door. The windows were the same scuffed, translucent plastic as the dome of the clock had been. Stopping at the glassed-in nurse's station, she went inside; around the corner, patients huddled in robes before a television set.

"God, of all the things to do!" I blurted out.

"You mean the TV?" she asked, sounding defensive. "Anyone can watch TV whenever they want. Some people can't sleep well, you know."

"But that stuff puts people here. What if everyone just gets sicker?"

"Were you a model or something?"

"Who said that?"

"Your chart."

"I worked as a model, but I wasn't one. I was an artist."

"Here's your daily schedule," the nurse said, pointing to the wall. Green felt-tip pen divided an orange construction-paper clock into neat sections. Each day followed the same plan: wake-up, medication, breakfast, group therapy, occupational therapy, lunch, individual therapy, rest, recreational therapy, dinner, medication, sleep.

"Don't you want to get in bed?" she asked. "You must be tired."

"I guess," I said, too exhausted to know.

I followed her to an empty room, watched her stack my inspected possessions on the top shelf of a metal locker, and crawled obediently into the small white bed. Pressing my head against the cool pillow, I ran my fingers over the nubby tufts of the chenille bedspread. I felt a sense of peace. After years of fighting, I'd finally admitted what I feared most—that I was hopelessly flawed, defeated, and helpless. . . . I wouldn't have to worry about my life anymore; I had an orange chart with felt-tip rules to follow. Every morning a nurse would peer through my scuffed window, glide noiselessly to my bed, and slip a glass thermometer from her silver tray into my mouth. Finally safe, as if I were in the heart of a lion, I slept.

Somebody to Love

It was night. Garnished in bright silk, satin, and feathers, people drifted through the warm December darkness. Alone in my car, I felt soothed and intoxicated by vodka and expectations. Laughter wafted like pale-colored smoke, and the hopeful energy sank into me. The contagious spirit made this concert by the Doors at the Shrine feel unique; it was time to get up my nerve and go backstage. My imperious attitude and embroidered clothes—a cross between a rich Russian and a biblical peasant in pants—led the doorman to believe I was a performer due onstage. Guilty at my deception, proud of the accomplishment, and saddened by how easily people are fooled by appearances, I walked inside.

As I drunkenly surveyed the auditorium, a woman onstage sang "Sometimes I Feel Like a Motherless Child." Weaving in and out of the crowd, I searched for a familiar face, though I was there only for Jim. I collided with Ronnie Krieger, the guitarist's brother, who was buying Cokes for the band. He seemed edgy until he saw I was, as usual, stoned on something, mysteriously giving me a reason for being there.

Soon we stood in the crowded dressing room, where I consumed enough grass and alcohol to numb myself against the uncomfortable banter of people appraising each other in a party that refused to begin. Anticipation etched the faces around me like mirrors; I wanted to hide. Finally, the door swung open, and Jim, looking the sulky dark angel, arrived. During this moment of total silence, the room paused, feeling his mood out for direction, waiting to see if he was willing to direct.

I donned a face of stony boredom, believing it allowed me to study Jim. While he talked, joked, and poured on the charm, he seemed to be searching for something. I didn't move a muscle or speak. In the middle of a conversation with a blond Englishman, Jim looked over at me and winked. It was very conspiratorial, as if we were sharing a great secret. I half smiled, not sure what I was being let in on. With a sudden rush, the band hurried off to perform. I trailed behind in a nervous stupor, finally sitting with Ronnie and Bill Siddons, the manager, by the stage.

Jim wasn't as loose as usual, perhaps recuperating from nearly falling off the stage the night before. Without that wild loss of control, he wasn't as convincing. His cries to tear down societal myths and taboos sounded guarded; no blurred, sweet smiles were passed to the other players. There was so little magic, I felt disappointed as the show came to an end. Soon everyone disbanded for home, and Jim mysteriously disappeared.

I collapsed into myself, purposeless as I walked to my car. I was really tired of trying to make him fall in love with me by pretending not to care, as if it were only by coincidence that my acid-induced ramblings had taken me backstage the past eleven months. My slickly incoherent version of a dumb blonde was wearing thin. I'd just finished high school six months before, but I was already exhausted from maintaining the stance of a pretty girl gone crazy from living in Newport Beach.

Reaching my car, I wanted to throw up or die. I sank down in the seat and rested my head against the steering wheel. The night filled with harsh droning as cars and people left the Shrine in a steady stream. The world grew silent and empty as I gazed across the vacant parking lot and contemplated the tedious job of driving back to my grandmother's place in Hollywood.

I heard footsteps and stifled laughter. My eyes refocused, and Jim filtered into view. Tall and deliberate, he walked alone, trying to look dignified—an impossibility while being followed by a group of giggling girls. They kept falling out of line and tugging at each other as he pretended not to notice. When he opened his car door, one girl jumped in the front seat, and another climbed on his lap and kissed him. Then a third traded places with the first.

The door slammed, Jim's car lurched into motion, and just as quickly, I followed him out of the parking lot. We drove down two dark blocks at a ridiculously slow pace until another car veered between us: another carload of girls. I tried to keep a discreet distance. He picked up speed, spun around a corner, and then slowed to a stop a few feet before the freeway entrance. Too late, I realized this was a trap, and I was caught.

Jim climbed out of his car, strolled leisurely down the ramp and chatted with the girls ahead of me. He glanced back at me with open amusement. It was hard to look aloof in these circumstances, but I tried. I studied the Felix the Cat Tire Store illuminating the corner with purple neon and frantically imagined I was an insomniac housewife pricing tires. I wasn't there for him; I wasn't one of those girls.

Slowly, elegantly, Jim stalked back to my car. Leaning over, he cast a sarcastic, what's-your-story look, shaking his head as if he'd caught me ruining my reputation. I glared back speechlessly.

"Are you following me?" he asked.

"I want to talk to you," I said in my most serious voice. I was in love with his soul; this was supposed to be a spiritual union, for God's sake.

"Aren't you going with Ronnie?" he asked skeptically.

"No. We're just friends. I mean, it's platonic."

"I asked, and everyone said you were going with him," he persisted. "At least that's what he thinks."

"Well, I'm not, at all." This was starting to seem too ordinary.

"That's different then," Jim said soothingly. "Why didn't you tell me? I'm living alone now, so why don't you come over?" His incredibly intimate, husky voice was aimed right at my ear. "I'm staying at a motel," he said, bending farther into the car. He'd obviously forgotten my line about wanting to talk.

"All right," I said.

"Just follow me. I can get rid of them—don't worry." He gave me a last, unneeded, seductive look and walked back to his car, this time ignoring the carload of girls. Watching him stride away like a great conquering lion, I wanted to start all over again. I'd thought I was going to conquer him, but he'd turned it around backward.

Even worse was my sense of anticlimax. The moon hadn't fallen from the sky; the earth hadn't cracked open. His songs happened in Egyptian deserts, Greek temples, moonlit roads leading to eternity. I was just following him over the Harbor Freeway to Hollywood. Pretty disappointing for two cosmic soul mates meeting again in the flesh.

Not only was I still in everyday reality, but I'd been caught in some kind of cops-and-robbers escapade. The carload of girls swerved manically from lane to lane, chasing Jim in bumper-to-bumper loops across the freeway. He pulled over to the side again, and a girl jumped out of his car. After she climbed back in the car with her friends, the parade launched on. As we finally pulled off the freeway onto Santa Monica Boulevard, a fire engine roared by. Jim stopped, his arm flung leisurely out the window as if he was watching the afternoon races. A few blocks later, the procession pulled into a liquor store parking lot. I leaned back my head, closed my eyes, and sighed.

"Don't fall asleep. We're almost there," Jim purred as he walked past me into the store. I turned to glare meaningfully at the girls. Surprisingly, their motor started up, and they disappeared into the night. Jim came out of the liquor store with his brown bag, apparently failed to notice his faithful fans had departed, and leaned into me, whispering, "It'll only be a few minutes now."

I wasn't that sure I wanted to do this anymore, but the voice inside warned I'd better or be sorry someday. We drove up a steep entrance under a bright neon arrow announcing the Alta Cieñega Motel in blue and red flashes. It was typically Californian, trying to give the illusion it was Spanish; withering green vines climbed around the rickety white lattices.

"It's upstairs," he said, nodding in the room's direction. Our footsteps echoed over the concrete as we climbed the stairs silently. Jim opened the door.

Once we were inside, I retreated into adolescence, dumbstruck as I stared at the bed. It was practically all the room was—a bed. I perched on the only chair, unable to recall my important reasons for being there. I couldn't say, "I never do these things"; he'd know how inexperienced I am. I couldn't say, "I'm a future famous artist, not just another girl"; he'd think I was nuts. My mind ranted in noisy desperation until I thought, He's the man; he should do something.

Jim drank his beer and contemplated the dusty curtains. I felt I was intruding or interrupting his thoughts, but my presence in the room slowly dawned on him. He put down his beer, walked over to me, and lightly placed his hands on my shoulders. Looking into my face, his eyes invited me to stand; his hands, moving to my waist, commanded it. I stood.

I wasn't exactly expecting a shot of beer in my mouth when he first kissed me. I almost choked, wondered if he wanted it back, and managed to swallow without coming up for a loud gulp of air. I even found this romantic; he was, after all, innovative. I'd just need more beer to soothe my nerves. . . . We regarded each other steadily, and he smiled shyly. After I finished off the bottle, we kissed again. His arms tightening around me, Jim pulled me closer, lifting me in a kind of unrushed passion.

Slightly more dramatic, he bent me back into a near swoon, pulling on my hair. It might've been OK if it had been my own hair, not a 100 percent human hair fall (the sixties precursor to hair extensions). The long blonde mass hung limply in his hand. I waited for him to start laughing or pointing, but he didn't. He acted as if everyone had two layers of hair; either that, or he wasn't interested in minor details. He just kept going. Reassured, I threw off my blouse in a gesture of bravery. Then I fell back on the bed and stared up at him.

Jim was onstage again, conscious of every movement. Undressing luxuriously, pausing every few seconds, he was beautiful to watch. Standing above me, his eyes holding mine intently, he slid the infamous black leather pants slowly down his pale, smooth skin. He moved softly down beside me. I lay there, mute and amazed.

Playful, he indulged in a tug-of-war game with my clothes. Once I was undressed, he rolled into a ball by my feet, examining my toes and ankles like a three-year-old discovering human anatomy. He did know the direct route up my legs, though, and his mood changed fluidly until he was moving slowly inside me, a sensual scientist searching and finding the right slants and curves. Keeping a quality of unhurried passion, he was lovely, mastering each sensation.

It was so easy, so perfect; it was like dreaming. I liked his back; it was smooth and solid. And I liked the way his shoulder blades veered out like wings, how fine and moist his skin felt. Touching him was like meeting who he really was, and I liked him more. It was much easier than talking. Surprised that he was what I expected, I assured myself that this really was Jim, his body next to mine.

LOVE HIM MADLY

I slipped into drowsiness and then rose to wakefulness again. I had to call my grandmother; she'd worry I was lying dead somewhere if I didn't.

"I have to make a phone call," I said reluctantly, jolting Jim back to reality.

"You'll have to go outside. There's not a phone in here," he said.

"That's all right." I felt relieved that he wouldn't hear me.

"Well, you'll have to put some clothes on then," he informed me. "I mean, I don't care, but they would. . . . It's probably cold out there, too."

"I know," I said, wondering if he thought I was without a brain. I threw on a combination of my clothes and his.

"If you can't stay, we'll get together another time soon." He sounded wistful and slightly hurt, but the casualness of his words stung. I had no intention of leaving, but I didn't want to explain that. Confused, I walked outside and made the call. I shivered as I lied to my grandmother Rosalie about staying with a friend, but my story was cheerfully accepted.

"Well?" Jim's voice sounded slightly anxious when I returned.

"I'm staying."

"Good," he said, half draping himself over me. Allowing himself a contented sigh, his breathing became deep, and without even the preface of a yawn, he fell fast asleep.

I lay wide awake, my mind racing. I had at least wanted to ask a few questions about his writing. . . . I pouted for a while, but without an audience it was useless. Finally, with dawn encroaching, I let myself fall asleep.

Break On Through

In the morning, Jim and I woke to the steady honking and hissing of traffic. Scared he wouldn't respond to me, I turned away nervously. He reached over, touched me, and without words, we made love. It seemed too automatic, and I felt hurt he wasn't talking, though I myself wouldn't speak. I was afraid it would seem too forward— of all the logic—I was naked in bed being shy.

Afterward, Jim stayed silent. He picked up a book, *The Origins and History of Consciousness*, and propped up our pillows. It was nonverbally understood we were going to sit up and read. At least, he was going to. My mind was too muddled to understand a complete sentence. The book was complex, full of complicated diagrams, illustrations, and endless annotations. I secretly just skimmed the captions and studied the pictures, pretending we were looking at sophisticated funny pages.

A million hours later, Jim slammed the book shut and pulled out a piece of notebook paper. He drew a circle and turned it into a kind of snake form, within which he created a woman's head with flying hair. This accomplished, he looked up at me. Apparently we were both deaf-mutes, so I just smiled and nodded agreeably. Maybe we were having some heavy metaphysical communication and I didn't know it. I did know I was nearly bursting with suppressed energy. To avoid having a fit, I climbed out of bed, quickly gathering my clothes as I walked into the bathroom.

In front of the mirror, I regained my self-control. While applying my mascara and blusher, I resigned myself to simply walking out, nodding good-bye, and forgetting any of this ever happened. When I reappeared with a ready-for-the-world air, Jim caught me off guard.

"What did you dream last night?" he asked, his urgent tone reducing me to honesty.

I stood, foiled midflight, trying to remember. "It was something about a fire that went out of control. It was really huge, and the water hoses wouldn't put out the flames." I shut up as quickly as I'd begun, embarrassed by the obvious symbolism.

He half smiled and motioned me to sit down by him in bed. He talked about dreams being interesting writing material and told me how he kept his in notebooks. Then he turned them into poems. I felt like I'd already read this somewhere, but I was glad we were at least talking. It was much more concrete than drawing pictures and using sign language.

I told him how alienated I'd felt from people lately, how hopelessly boring, numb, and dead everybody seemed. "I mean, everyone just seems so mediocre!" I concluded. I waited patiently for Jim to save me from this dilemma. Out of pride, I didn't mention his songs had almost made these problems appear, so only he could make them disappear.

"Alienation is a bad one. . . ." He mulled this over for a while. "I guess most people really are mediocre," he agreed in a surprised, sorry voice. To my horror, it sounded as if he'd never noticed this before.

"Well, doesn't it bother you or anything?" I asked, shifting impatiently.

"When I was younger, I was more idealistic. I always thought it was just a matter of time, you know, before I had a lot of friends, close friends who were doing the same thing as me. But it never happened." It looked like this had just hit him. "The other guys in the band are like brothers, you know, brothers. . . . I mean, I like them, we work well together, but we're not really alike." Jim stopped reflectively, as if burdened by an old dream.

"I'm really glad the hair on your legs is light," I said idiotically. "I was really afraid it might be black." I didn't add I was also glad he didn't have skinny toothpick legs like my girlfriend Linda predicted. It was bad enough that he didn't have any friends and was young such a long time ago.

"Did you know my hair is really red?" Jim asked brightly, cocking his head sideways so I could really tell.

"It is not. It's dark brown."

"No, it's red! There are all kinds of red highlights and streaks in it. It just looks brown. You could tell if we were in the sun—it's actually red," he said.

God, I could just imagine him out in the sun, hunting for red strands with a mirror. This really irritated me, since his main girlfriend, Pam, had real red hair, not just highlights.

"You've really got a thing about red hair, don't you?" I asked, wanting to get up and leave.

"Well, I just think it's sort of rare." He pronounced "rare" in a slighted, defensive way and looked at me distrustfully, as if rare things were beyond me.

"Don't you think it's weird that you're famous?" I said, now that I was being uncouth.

"I just think it was a coincidence," Jim said, as if I were interviewing him. "Something just comes along at the right time, and it happens. We never thought it would be a hit. You know, I wrote the music and Robby wrote the lyrics. Everybody always forgets that." Seeming impressed by these facts, he pulled the sheets up around his neck.

"People get all needy and greedy looking when you get to the 'We want the world and we want it now' part of 'When the Music's Over,'" I told him. "I mean, they practically go crazy."

"Yeah, I know." He sighed morosely. "What lyrics do you like?"

"'The face in the mirror won't stop / The girl in the window won't drop / A feast of friends, alive, she cried.'" Feeling pretty stupid reciting lyrics, I stopped and recrossed my legs. They were getting numb. "And the 'scream of the butterfly' part," I added.

"Yeah, I like that. 'A feast of friends.' I like the way that sounds . . . 'a feast of friends.'" Jim went off into a rhapsody of contemplation.

"Don't you get sick of people turning all silent and stuff just because you walk into a room?"

"Yeah, I never expected that." He sighed, a weighted-down, heavy sigh. "It even seems to affect my intimate friends," he drawled, looking at me too meaningfully for comfort. I remained silent. "You stood out a lot more in a crowd when your hair was really blonde," he said. It seemed mildly offensive that he would prefer my dumb-blonde persona, especially after I'd so worked hard to remove it.

"Probably . . . but it almost made me crazy. This one time, I was coming onto acid in this lavender gas-station bathroom—in one of those freeway-exit cities. And I just couldn't stand my hair being phony anymore. After that, I had to have it dyed back to natural."

"You have to be careful with acid," Jim said. "It shouldn't be misused. You should just take it at the right times, when you really mean it." He sounded so reverent about the whole thing that I wondered if he was making fun of me. But he stayed all holy looking, so I started feeling guilty about all the wrong times I'd taken acid.

"I thought your performance was better the first night. You were so much looser," I said. Our conversation was so disconnected; we made it better as deaf-mutes.

"That's interesting. I thought so, too." He sat up straighter. "I like performing that way. It's better. But everyone else said it was too loose! That I was too loose. I don't know—that's just the way I am." Jim shrugged, hurt, as if he was constantly misunderstood. He moved closer to me and cupped his hands over my breasts, his fingers lightly tracing over my cotton blouse. "Why did you really want to see me?" he asked, lowering his voice to utter secrecy.

"I've had this kind of obsession about you. For a really long time. I always identified with you, I guess. Like you were really me," I said, admitting the truth.

"You mean, you think if you were a man, you'd be me?"

"Well, yeah, sort of . . ." I'd never taken it to that extreme, but maybe it was the logical conclusion.

"That's very interesting," he said. I couldn't believe this "interesting" reaction he had to everything. He kept looking at my face, imagining it transformed, I guess. I thought he'd be much more opinionated.

"I'm going to art school in the fall," I announced in a rush of confidence, considering I hadn't been accepted yet.

He raised an eyebrow. "Where?"

"Chouinard Art Institute."

Jim nodded appreciatively, continuing to trace circles around my breasts. The cloth made odd crinkling noises beneath his fingers. "You're so self-contained," he said, making it seem both a compliment and complaint.

"What do you mean, 'self-contained'?" It sounded like I was a jar of preserves.

"You're self-contained. Like you're within yourself, self-sufficient and self-confident."

"Oh. Usually people can't tell. I'm too quiet and it doesn't show," I said. Jim leaned his head back, studying my face. Embarrassed and over-explained, I looked down at my hands. He took one hand and looked at the gold chain-link ring on my finger.

"It's a good one," he said gently, looking from the ring to my eyes. Jim slipped the ring off my finger and put it on his. Holding out his hand, he surveyed the effect and smiled uncertainly. I was silent, feeling his somber mood as he slid the ring off his finger and back onto mine.

"It's getting late," he finally said.

"I know. I have to go."

Filled with unexpected pain, I rested my head against his chest for a moment. I was bursting and suffocating with sudden knowledge that I could never have him—he was not something to have. Torn between a desire to ask for help or run away, I started to cry, hoping he'd see my tears.

"I think we'll be good friends now, don't you?" he asked, tenderly holding me back at arm's length.

"Yes," I murmured.

"I really don't have many. I'm so glad this happened," he continued. "I'll be gone ten days on tour, but give me your number now, and I'll call as soon as I'm back. OK?"

I nodded and mechanically wrote down my number. Shyly avoiding his eyes, I picked up my purse and headed for the door.

"Do you have your hair?" Jim asked, smirking.

"It's in my purse," I said, laughing involuntarily.

"See you later," he said huskily.

The promise lingered as I left him. Downstairs in the daylight, I remembered it was Christmas Eve. And I'd never told him my name. I wondered about the man lying naked and alone in his motel room. I knew I couldn't go back, so I wrote a note: "Jim, I didn't tell you, but my name is Judy." I left it under his windshield wipers and drove away.

Fire and Rain

Dr. Atkins, my ex-hippie psychiatrist, led me down a long, dingy corridor to his office. He unlocked the door with a key from the jangling keychain on his Levi's belt loop and smiled sheepishly. "We're in a locked ward, but you're not really locked in. You can always leave whenever you want," he'd explained. It was a point I didn't quite understand, a safety issue. Inside, his office was small and neat, pale grayish green. Behind his battle-scarred desk, the barred window overlooked a cement courtyard. The mental patients actually had a basketball hoop down there.

Once we were seated, he studied me with myopic brown eyes. "Last night, I found it interesting that you barely mentioned your family. Your problems as an artist, feminism, and a lover's death are important, but you must have been depressed before. What was it like growing up?"

Immediately, I felt prickly, irritated that he would be so reductive—no wonder there was a picture of Freud on the wall. "I don't think that's the problem. I'm an only child, so there wasn't anyone. I mean, except my parents. And they've been divorced for a long time, since I was sixteen."

"What was that like?"

"I was glad," I said, a bit too defiantly. "All they did was fight. I kind of made my mom leave because he was such a tyrant."

"You made your mother leave your father. You don't think she would have left anyway?"

"I don't think so. My dad was so strict; he grounded me for everything. He held up glasses I washed to the light, and if there were any streaks, I got grounded. He inspected my bedroom, too. But the real thing was . . . he hated all my boyfriends."

"How does that make you feel today?" Dr. Atkins asked.

"Mad. It felt like my fault, like I was wrong. And that just made me madder. It seemed like I was betraying him. Then I started liking boys a lot."

"Did that seem related—the boys and your father?"

"That seems pretty dumb. And over-Freudian," I said, glancing scornfully at the grumpy old man on his wall.

On that indeterminate day in the midseventies, the sixties finally ended. Seasons and years had blurred. It wasn't fall or summer; it was early spring or winter. It must have been April: a gloomy, gray month, dawn without color. I could remember nothing but rain on Melrose Avenue, trucks and wet tires drowning out birdsong. I dealt tarot cards until early morning, smoking pot as I wrote: "Swords, swords, swords; you rule war. I cut off my long hair; it wouldn't grow past my shoulders for a decade."

I'd carefully applied eye makeup and curled my hair under at the ends before Mom drove me to the psychiatric hospital at County/USC. I wore leather platform sandals, skinny dark jeans, a bat-wing blouse with an Aztec pattern, and a huge shell necklace. I clutched a folded doctor's note from Southern California Counseling Center recommending immediate inpatient treatment, but I didn't want anyone to think I was crazy.

After all, I had come back from Paris; I had seen Jim's grave. Now even his girlfriend, Pam, had OD'd. My first book had been rejected, my suicide attempts had failed, and I dreamed of killing my mother. I was too disdainful of modeling to succeed at that, ruining Plan C for surviving after a BFA from California Institute of the Arts. Fine art had concrete limits, as fame did; my time was up. I'd gone twenty-four years without a break. This was my break.

Once I'd been admitted, I actually took the inkblot test I'd heard about in movies and books; soon I might progress to the territory featured in *Sybil*, *Lilith*, or *The Three Faces of Eve*. The Rorschach had plenty of carnivorous animals, caves, knives, and blood: "He's trying to devour her, but she can stab him with that sword." It was clearly one long narrative of sexism and my parents' divorce.

Dr. Atkins asked me to explain certain sayings: for instance, people who live in glass houses shouldn't throw stones.

"You'd break your own house," I said impatiently.

"A rolling stone gathers no moss?"

"You're going too fast for anything to stick . . . like people."

"Haste makes waste."

"You just make a mess if you hurry," I said. The meanings seemed so obvious that I felt irritated. Fortunately, he switched to word association, backward numbers, and the naming of continents, of which I could only remember five. Antarctica and Australia had fallen off my globe.

Dr. Atkins informed me I was a "romantic idealist" with good abstract-thinking skills but little or no practical or mechanical ability. This unfortunate combo created a double whammy—it would be difficult to live in the world like that. My IQ didn't count for much; furthermore, the MMPI (Minnesota Multiphasic Personality Inventory) tests reported that I'd "psyched them out," so the results weren't reliable. A deflating start—the world itself was flat.

Oh, well—time for lunch! The food was a blur, except for the graham crackers and milk. I trusted the little cardboard boxes of cereal. Everything else seemed dehydrated: mashed potatoes, eggs, and hamburger patties. Food caught steaming inside the plastic trays smelled so odd that I contracted further inward. Over the long metal tables, windows with wire netting filtered out the sun, keeping the room obliquely shaded. Fuzzy gray light refracted off the blaring TV, solidifying the heavy feeling in my chest.

I wouldn't always be sitting next to some crazy who ranted in front of Canter's on Fairfax between hospitalizations. A perfectly nice person, too. We watched the flickering tube as the black nurses laughed at Joan Collins; it was hearty laughter; they clearly appreciated her. I reached for a carton of chocolate milk. But the gray windows, the green walls pressed in on me. Apparently there was no escape.

When I Was Young

I had arranged to stay with my grandmother Rosalie in Hollywood for the two evenings I was attending the Doors concerts at the Shrine. When nothing happened the first night, I returned to her apartment defeated. She knew I'd had a crush on a singer for months and shared my enthusiasm that we would finally talk.

"There are so many things I want to ask him about," I told her. "I just have to know him."

"You will, dear," she assured me.

It was a strange mix of her old-fashioned world and mine as I'd dressed in her bathroom the next night. The rooms smelled of roses, mothballs, Lily of the Valley perfume, Noxzema, and pumpkin pie spice. Ivory linen, lace, and a silver hand mirror lay across her dressing table next to sepia photographs of my mother as a girl in Iowa. In the front room, Christmas cards and holly surrounded an oval photo of my grandfather, who watched over everything as if he were a shrine.

Rosalie had become a nurse after my grandfather died decades before in a train accident; she usually wore a starched white uniform. She'd learned to take care of herself, without anyone's help, and often carried her nurse's overnight bag. It was like her—sturdy and familiar, humble yet confident, practical and capable. When I saw it sitting on the floor by itself, I somehow felt it was her.

Rosalie had her own beliefs, and I found them comforting. She rarely talked about them to my parents, so nobody could disagree. Every year before Christmas, she'd come to my room at bedtime, carefully closing the door so only a tiny filter of light shone through the crack. Her plump body hovered near, brushing against mine like the fluttering wing of a bird. She'd gently tuck in my covers, sit down, and take my hand in hers, the skin warm and soft as her voice. "The Lord is my shepherd," she began, "I shall not want."

As a child, I found comfort in the fact that Rosalie knew her prayers by heart. She said them so simply and surely that they felt like truth sinking into me, like her mist of perfume did. My room would transform into a quiet sanctuary, a candlelit world of sepia shadows burning with the small holy light. "Surely goodness and mercy shall follow me all the days of life," the prayer would end, but I wished it could last forever. Now, as Rosalie baked pies before I left for the Doors concert, I studied myself in her full-length mirror and decided, This is it. I have to be with him. It has to be tonight.

When I left Jim at the Alta Ciénega motel that Christmas Eve morning, I had to drive only a few blocks to pick up Rosalie in West Hollywood. The streets were gray and emptying; the sad tinsel and greenery on lampposts on Santa Monica Boulevard seemed touching, like an oversized red bow on a dog. Almost delirious, I rushed into her little blue bungalow, inhaling the familiar scents of cinnamon, camphor, and Noxzema. As if for the first time, I saw the romantic vision of my handsome, ageless grandfather watching from her mantel. I knew him only from that large sepia-toned photograph. With luminous eyes set in deep sockets, high cheekbones and forehead, my grandfather looked like a saint, poet, or philosopher. A tangible presence in her home, his benevolent, watchful gaze presided from her horizontal mirror. Even though he'd died when my mom was seven, Rosalie had explained she was still married to him and always would be. It was understood that she'd see him again someday.

"What was he like, Rosalie?" I'd asked again that weekend. "Did you know from the start?"

"I did. Whatever anyone says, there is love at first sight. And I knew. . . . He was a true gentleman, kind and sensitive. Things took longer then . . . cars and telephones were new . . ."

We didn't talk of his death much. Sometimes, as I grew older, she would cry if we'd been talking about him. But not today.

"Jim and I were together!" I exulted as she sat down in her rocker. "We talked—we really talked. He likes me—I know he does!"

Rosalie knew enough not to question exactly what had happened and seemed happy just to know I was. We seemed more linked than before. I could have a love like she'd had, one that transcended time, life, and death, a love that would be eternal. Hadn't I always known?

Hadn't I loved him in another life? Wouldn't he be different from every guy, everyone I'd ever known?

"He's everything I've always wanted," I said, driving Rosalie to Corona del Mar, where I lived with my mother.

When my parents divorced two years before, Mom found a cute, furnished duplex about five minutes down Coast Highway from Dad in Newport Beach. Since she had been the unfaithful one, she refused alimony and began to work. Our years of frozen dinners had begun: Swanson TV dinners and Chicken Delight. We claimed to like them better, and for a while, it was true. My dad hadn't liked them, but they were delicious; why bother cooking? I loved pulling back the thin silver foil to reveal perfect apple crisps, mashed potatoes, or miniature blueberry muffins. Overnight, slaving over the hot stove became a thing of the past. In fact, she'd never return to cooking beyond an occasional steak and potato.

Mom had once loved my dad's wild sense of humor; when they met, he was a fun-loving musician. Though he was no longer singing with Frank Sinatra and the Pied Pipers, he had still sung on the radio, TV, and occasionally in the movies. But when things got tough, she was more willing to face the financial instability of a musician's life than the dull security of the real estate salesman he'd become. Already heavy social drinkers, they began their alcoholic drinking in earnest.

As a toddler in Hollywood, I'd seen my father singing on Rosalie's new TV set and blurted out hello. I stumbled toward the screen, one hand reaching out. Dad seemed to gaze at me from inside the big gray box, but he didn't answer. Mom and Rosalie laughed and explained he couldn't see or hear me. I supposed they were telling the truth but hoped he would tell me differently later. Of course, he didn't. But the incident made an impression, forming my desire to capture that illusion.

I used to study my parents' wedding pictures, my only clues to the unfathomable life they had before me. I flipped the heavy album pages slowly. My mother stood tall and erect, as she had as a model, and cut the cake with Dad, who seemed intent on getting the shot just right. Between them floated Rosalie's face and her hand, clasping my mother's sleeve—what was that? Some kind of a warning? I felt the frustrated depth of my parents' longing, the illusive ideal they were striving for but only seemed to lose, though their dream stayed buried in my heart.

"This is the best Christmas I've had! Being with Jim was the best present I could ever have," I repeated to Rosalie and my mother as we ate our holiday dinner. Christmas 1967 was our third with only the three of us, without Dad and his family.

"I hope it works out, honey," they both told me, smiling at different times.

Only now do I wonder if they were truly cheerful or carefully guarded. I wonder if they could have known or if they could they have stopped me. And if I had known, would I have stopped myself? Could I have?

Backdoor Man

Christmas 1967 was the last entry in my teenage diaries. My small, colored books with narrow lines, locks, and keys were nothing like the large blank journals I'd begin. I wrote in one entry, "I can only say how beautiful he is. I told him everything and he understands. I knew he would. . . . If this works out, I will be so happy it almost seems unfair. Someone I really love that really understands and can teach me everything. I would be so lucky." Yes, he could teach me a few things—and what a teacher.

As 1968 began, I stayed at home with my mom, my books, and my dog. In this safety zone, I became deluded as hell. Now that I'd "officially" met Jim, I imagined the love affair of all had begun; the gods of truth and justice would reward my unswerving devotion. I floated along in a blissful daze, unfazed by my girlfriends' warnings. Knowing I was asking for something that could never be, I cast all reason to the wind. And with that reckless gesture, I became irretrievable. I crossed the line and waited for a golden call that never came.

One morning in January, I got up and dressed, supposedly for my art class at Orange Coast College. It seemed a little strange to choose a silk blouse, a brocade vest, a miniskirt, and my best boots for class, but I told myself I was just thinking of visiting Jim. I managed to maintain that vague point of view all the way from the beach to Hollywood. By the corner of La Ciénega and Santa Monica Boulevard, it became clear I wasn't going to class. My heart found its way into my throat, pounding wildly offbeat, making it hard to breathe and even harder to think. I relied on automatic pilot to get me to the motel. After parking and turning off the engine, I lost my momentum. I just sat there, watching the shiny blue metal of his Mustang glint in the sun.

Eventually, I convinced myself I'd better do something. I looked in the mirror, climbed out of the car, and stood purposelessly. That just made things worse, since I was visible and someone might see me standing there, dumbstruck. Walking down the sloping parking lot in a blind panic, I bumped into an angry manager.

"What do you want?" he demanded.

"Nothing. I don't want anything. I just came to see someone, you know. He's just staying here."

"Who?" The man looked me up and down as if I was an underage hooker or junkie, or both.

"Jim Morrison."

"Mr. Morrison is not to be disturbed until three in the afternoon. He doesn't get up until then." His tone implied I was a dubious character if I didn't know these basics. "Mr. Morrison is a very busy man."

"Oh, OK, I'll just wait then." I gratefully slunk back to the security of my car, supposedly to wait until three, though it wasn't even noon yet. I counted the bricks on the wall, using different systems, tried to calculate how many bricks I could count per minute, how many hours it would take to count the entire wall, and how many times I'd count it before Jim came out of his room . . .

A door slammed, an engine revved, shiny blue metal glinted in the sun—and I jolted to life. It was him. I nearly fell out of my car, and then I nonchalantly walked over to his. The late morning air was moist and clean from the night's rain. Jim rolled down his window and smiled up at me. I'd never seen anything so beautiful as his face, gentle in that light, calm, almost radiant. I couldn't speak.

"Hello, Judy." He said my name softly, sounding amused, possessed of himself.

"Hi," I croaked, about to keel over but acting cool.

"This is a nice surprise," Jim drawled. "I'm just going over to Elektra for a little while. Do you want to come along with me?"

I looked down at particles of black gravel caught in the deep grooves of his front tire. This brief hesitation caused Jim to quickly reconsider.

"Oh, never mind, you'd probably get bored. It'll be faster if I go alone. Will you wait for me?"

"Yeah," I said.

"OK, I'll hurry and be right back. Here's my room key. Don't let anyone inside but me," Jim said as he handed me the key. "See you soon," he promised and drove away.

He'd changed rooms. This one was larger and more lived-in. Magazines were flung open across the floor, books fell from stacks like playing cards, and scraps of notebook paper were scattered all over the dresser. "They're all scared," was scrawled darkly by his nightstand. That meant me, too, I realized guiltily. I was even afraid to read his black journal, though it was inches from my hand. Either it would be bad karma, or he'd catch me.

I sat gingerly on the edge of his bed and picked up *The Tibetan Book of the Dead*, in hopes of distancing reality by making it cosmic. Reading a paragraph, I imagined golden-rose molecular light exploding as my soul left my body. Then the maid walked in, scaring me into the corner chair. Shaking out a pillowcase, she smiled hopefully.

"Are you an actress?" she asked.

"No, I'm an artist. I paint," I answered.

She looked at me with mild disappointment. "Is he an actor?"

"No, he's mostly a singer. And he writes," I added apologetically. I watched words swim across the page in swirling black patterns as she changed sheets, dusted, and replaced towels in an efficient flurry. She left as quickly as she'd come, meeting my eyes with a timid smile that made me sad.

I read intently, preparing to meet Jim on a higher plane, though I'd been drawn to him mindlessly. Jim was youth—male beauty and grace and a delicate destructibility, and he was riding a cold, merciless wave of passion. I loved him for that—for living impossibly rather than dying in slow, aching degrees. He had become my glorified inner self made public.

By the time I heard Jim's whistle approaching, I'd disintegrated to vapor, more prepared to discuss the relative degrees of death than to kiss him. I was a floating cloud of white light when he knocked on the door, and I let him in. He threw his arms around me, kissed me hard and passionately, bombarding me with raw sexuality. He was a good kisser, slow and dreamy and fierce all at once. We were floating into another world where everything was perfect; I was born to do this. Just to kiss. But my spine froze as he turned to double-lock the door. I felt rooted by gravity. Much as I'd sought him out, I didn't know how to take him.

"Oh, God, my boots are killing me," Jim said, collapsing backward on the bed. "Please take them off," he said, rocking forward. Eyes cracked half-open, he looked like a disobedient child trying not to smile as he purposely made his legs dead weight. He propped himself up on his elbows and helped by turning his ankles inward. Showing more cooperation when I reached his leather pants, he easily arched his body away from the bed. His right hand paused lightly on the nape of my neck, grasped my hair by the roots, and slowly pulled me up beside him.

"Let me undress you now," he said somberly, holding me at arm's length. He removed each piece of my clothing, folding it meticulously before moving to the next. When we were both naked, he seemed to coil and strike sudden as a snake, and I lay stunned on my back. His black-framed angel face rose above me, seeming both innocent and corrupt, good and evil, looking down upon our bodies locked below.

"Tell me you want me to fuck you."

"I want you to fuck me," I mumbled, as if reading a script I didn't understand.

"Say it like you mean it!" he demanded.

"I want you to fuck me."

"Good. That's good. Now tell me you love it—you love me to fuck you."

LOVE HIM MADLY

"I love you to fuck me," I murmured, reverting to my bad actress role.

"Come on. Tell me. You love it. Don't you?"

"Yes," I whispered.

"Then tell me."

"I love you to fuck me."

"Come on, I said tell me!"

As I reluctantly repeated the words, Jim's face fluctuated rapidly, changing essence until a cold, wild element tyrannized the others. The black line curving above his upper lip seemed darker, taunting, accentuating the menacing edge in his voice. "Have you ever been fucked in the ass?"

"Yes." I tried to sound pleasant but bored.

"I want to fuck you in the ass."

"I didn't really like it that much. I don't really want to. Don't, OK?" Too late—I knew he'd seen my fear and felt contempt.

"I want to," he hissed, hollowing me to the marrow. He had snapped.

Jim's eyes looked black, blazing with hatred or defiance. I was afraid he was going to hit me, slap me, shake me. He pinned down my arms, flat against the bed. I was watching a movie I was acting in, but he was directing. He seemed so crazy that I realized he could kill me. And something died, dropped out of me. The surroundings blurred, my boundaries were lost, and nothing was left but his brutal need driving out of control, until I realized he was raping me.

I twisted beneath him, suddenly lashing out for survival, clawing and yelling at him to stop. Almost as abruptly, he stopped. His eyes registered surprise, widened back to blue, and filled with tenderness, focusing on me as if I was a child he loved dearly. Still holding his weight on my forearms, he leaned over and sadly kissed my forehead and mouth. Wistful longing played across his face as he looked straight into my eyes and gently traced my cheekbones with his fingers. I stared back, bruised with incomprehension.

"I'm going to take a shower now," Jim said in a polite voice. "Come on in, if you want." Staring at the ceiling, I remained motionless. I tried to fathom what had happened; the boyfriends I'd had before wouldn't have done this. After a few minutes, I realized he wasn't coming back to comfort me. Waiting for an apology would only humiliate me further, so I got up.

I found Jim washing his hair and whistling, in a great mood. He smiled tentatively as I got in, picked up the soap and covered my body with white lather. Then he stood back so the hot water ran down my body, temporarily proving himself kind and considerate. As the soap slid smoothly between us, he kissed me sweetly. Then he lathered me up again, smiling childishly.

"I'm going to dry off. But stay inside if you want." Jim casually turned off the hot water as he got out, so a hard stream of icy water attacked me.

"What'd you do that for?" I demanded, jumping out.

"I don't know, I just thought it might be kind of . . . exhilarating." His bright smile flickered to disappointment as I gazed accusingly at him. Tossing me a clean towel, he left the bathroom.

I was drawn through the steam to the mirror to see how I looked—or if I was still there. As I wiped off the mist, I saw my hair was unevenly drenched and badly disarrayed. Even worse, my mascara had run in diluted black swirls down my face.

"I look like Frankenstein," I said in horror, without thinking. This was the final indignity. My physical self, the only thing I could rely on, was gone, obliterated. Only after repeatedly scrubbing my face and rewetting and combing my hair was I ready to face him again.

Jim sat by the window, looking cool and collected in his white towel. Sighing, I collapsed dramatically on the bed. "Would you like a beer?" he asked, looking worried.

"Yeah, I need something," I muttered.

"There's a store right around the corner. I can just walk over and get some." Jim put on a pair of faded corduroy pants and an old V-neck sweater, appearing quite likable and unthreatening out of black leather or bed. He looked just like any other hippie, until he walked. Casting me a nervous glance, he gently shut the door as if the slightest noise might shatter me. Seconds out of range, he started whistling.

I threw on my clothes, reapplied mascara, and struggled to compose my mind. Maybe I was naive and should give him another chance. Despite the evidence, I didn't want to believe he was as dangerous or destructive as some people said. I still wanted to find out what he was really like. When Jim returned, I'd pulled myself together, no longer pouting or expecting an apology.

"I didn't mean to hurt you," he said, handing me a Miller.

"I know," I answered, feeling calmer as I swallowed the beer. The truth remained but was easily dismissed.

Drinking helped Jim relax, too. He talked in an easy, drifting way.

"You know, it's weird. A couple of months ago, I was at the Fillmore, and I was singing 'The End' . . . and I'd really gotten into it, you know. I'd forgotten about everything else—I really meant it. And then something happened. For some reason, I opened my eyes. I don't usually even see people, but there were these people in the front row. And they were laughing at me. Like I was funny!"

Jim picked up his beer, studied his hands, and glanced at me, baffled and hurt. "It's like they won't take me seriously; they don't want to, even when I'm serious. I think they make me a fool."

Before I could answer, there was a knock on the door.

"Who is it?" Jim asked irritably.

"It's a secret!" It was a playful, lilting girl's voice.

"Come on—who is it?"

"It's me!" she chirped.

"Oh, sweetheart," Jim crooned.

"Sapphire!" she exclaimed, delighted. I guessed this was an *Amos 'n Andy* comedy they had going and felt even more left out. "Hey, aren't you going to let me in?"

"I don't have any clothes on now. Why don't you come back later?"

"Jim, I came all the way down here, and now you won't let me in?" She sounded so shocked. I wondered where she had come down from.

"Now, Pam, sweetheart. I'm busy. Can't you just come back in a little while?"

"Jiiiiim!" Pam cried, outraged. I imagined her big green eyes growing wider in angry disbelief, her petite body raging, the long red hair streaming down her back. "Jim, I know there's someone in there with you. I just know it!"

Jim rolled his eyes and shrugged. He put his finger to his lips and motioned me back against the wall. "Well, anyway, like I was saying, I couldn't understand what those people wanted. Of course, you know those people in San Francisco . . . but New York's bad, too." He shook his head.

"Jim, you're disgusting. I can't believe you're doing this again! If you don't let me in, I'm leaving," Pam screamed.

"I've been thinking of taking some time off soon," Jim said to me. I couldn't move my face muscles. I was pretending it was a radio melodrama, but I felt slaughtered and at their mercy.

"Jim, listen, if you come out now, I'll roast leg of lamb for dinner. And you have to come see my new apartment. Besides, I'll take you on your errands, so you won't have to drive. Jim?"

"I'm sorry, honey. I just don't know what to do. See, there's this crazy girl in here. She's just lying here on the bed with her legs open. What should I do?"

"Jim, this is it! I'm leaving!"

"But, Pam, sweetheart, you should understand, she's your sister, Judy. You shouldn't be mad."

"I know we're all in the same family and everything. I just want to see what she looks like!"

"It's too bad we don't have a back door. That's one of the bad things about this place." Warming to his bizarre talk-show host role, he grinned. I slipped on a mask of aloof amusement.

"Jim, let me in! I want to see her!" Pam beat on the door with her fists and screamed. "Let me see her!" I felt like a piece of meat, waiting to be hung and inspected for flaws.

"Now, Pam . . . I think it'd be best if you just get in your little car and drive home," Jim reasoned.

"Jim, help me! The maid's screaming at the manager, and they're coming. Let me in!"

Pam's hysteria reached a crescendo with renewed door pounding, shrieking, broken Spanish, shattered glass, and masculine knocks on the door. Forced into decisive action, Jim reached for his jacket and nodded solemnly toward the bathroom door.

"Lock it," he whispered, handing me another beer. Grabbing my purse, I fled to safety.

"Get together, one more time," Jim sang. "Get together, one more time," he continued, walking out the door.

I could hear voices locked in anger, more pounding and screaming. I rested my head against the cool bathroom tiles and closed my eyes. Sounds rose and fell around me, gradually muffled into buzzing silence. I curled into a fetal position on the floor with my slightly warm beer. I waited a long time; when I was sure they had gone, I got up and walked in slow, listless circles. I noticed my blood, bright on the clean bedspread, and hoped it would make a nice conversation piece when they returned. Torn between writing "I hate you" across the walls and leaving my number so he could apologize, I did neither. I left.

I Am a Rock

I still can't remember exactly what happened after I left that motel. It felt like I'd been run over by a truck, just flattened. Everything was far away, shot from a long lens in a movie . . . except for the close-ups of bright red on my underwear. That seemed like proof. I never told anyone what happened. I just said I'd seen Jim, and Pam came, and he left. That was bad enough. I couldn't find the words; I was too ashamed. And I couldn't really understand it. That look on his face, the way he just turned on me, took over . . . it seemed like a mistake, something I had to change. And if it wasn't a mistake, then I was somehow wrong inside, and no one would ever love me. The worst thoughts I'd ever had about myself would be true. It hurt too much to feel that, so I just kind of blanked it out. I went back to my classes and doing portfolio pieces to get into art school. It's funny, because I was in a psychology class, too, modeled after the Esalen encounter groups. No one there had a clue what I was feeling—least of all me. But it seemed like God was gone.

White Rabbit

A few weeks after the episode with Jim, I found myself in a solitary cell at the Sybil Brand Penal Institute for Women—it seemed to be the mentally disturbed division. All I could remember was watching a movie in which I played a character about to be executed. If it was only a movie, why was I in jail? If it was real, why was I still alive? My face was bluish and bloated, covered with angry red blotches. My wrists were raw, swollen crimson. Every few minutes, someone flashed a light in my eyes. Obviously, this was a new reality. I wove the hazy threads of memory back together.

My girlfriend Patty and I had driven up into the mountains, but halfway there, we'd lost our bearings. Patty decided we'd better get her boyfriend, Ray, to take us to a safe place. Under the influence of purple Owsley acid, I easily agreed. As we sped down the mountain road, each winding curve brought laughter and joy at being alive and within the hands of nature. Faces radiated from the cliffs, sending timeless love and wisdom. I felt a reckless, soaring grace, and my life dropped behind me, perfectly justified; it was just the past.

Then the flying stopped, and we crashed back to earth. In front of a flashing red light at a railroad crossing, the shriek of the approaching train welled up inside me. Toying with the small ivory cross around her neck, Patty looked curiously at me. Colored alphabets formed words across her face as she spoke.

"Jim must be pretty strange," she said, forcing my disowned past back into the present. "I mean that one line, 'Women seem wicked when you're unwanted'?" Reflective blue-gray eyes studied me from her pale, cameo face. "That's a pretty heavy thing for a man to say." She smoothed back her long red hair and rolled her eyes. "And those pants he wears . . . What's he really like?"

Her voice was a cool murmur, a distant waterfall, as my mind screeched in panic. I didn't want to remember Jim. The train roared past, endless and ugly in the harsh, grating light. I studied the translucent skin barely shielding the blue veins of my wrist. Vivid and strong, my pulse beat naked and vulnerable; I could feel the blood rush. The veins on my wrist are Jim, I thought, and I remembered what happened. I had to change it.

"I have to go see him," I said, resolutely shifting the car forward.

"Judy, I think you ought to wait a while first. This stuff is pretty strong."

"But I have to see him!"

"At least wait until we see Ray. We really shouldn't be driving around like this. He'll know what to do." Patty had assumed the firm, feminine logic of her mother, watching me as if I was about to plunge over the edge.

"OK, I'll wait," I said. Discontent rose and stuck in my throat.

We were back in the city. Brash neon lights glowed through the congested air. Though the midday sun glared down from the ashen sky, it looked like twilight. Particles of fine toxic dust settled into my pores. When the traffic lights changed, people seemed fanatically serious about dashing to the next red light. I suspected they had rigid rules of conduct and tried to mold my face into complacent obedience, but my features felt too elastic to control.

We'd reached our goal: the parking lot of a pool hall in West Covina, where Patty could find her boyfriend.

"God, it's really intense out there," she said. "Do you mind if we just sit here a while? I'm not ready to see Ray yet."

"Yeah," I said. "It's pretty creepy here." There was a beauty supply store, a pastrami sandwich shop, a Laundromat, and a dog grooming shop. I'd spent so much time in parking lots; I realized I'd probably die in a parking lot.

"We probably should've stayed in the mountains, but I was afraid we needed Ray. So we wouldn't get lost, you know?" Patty shrugged apologetically. I nodded, relieved the city had affected her adversely, too, and started to trust her again in a small, tentative way. "You're not mad at me?" she asked.

"Not really." Softening, I smiled. Then I giggled. "Look at that woman over there—she looks like a Saint Bernard!"

"Judy, that's not a woman. It is a Saint Bernard!"

Sitting behind the steering wheel, the dog stared out, a mournful parody of the people we had seen. Patty and I collapsed in hysterics. Laughing, I suddenly felt as purified as I had in the mountains. A radiant light broke through the sky, cutting a path down toward us. With ethereal notes of music, a golden luminosity filtered through clouds and smog, bathing even the oil-stained pavement, dusty cars, and dingy buildings with such forgiving beauty. I started to cry.

"God, everything is so beautiful! You're so beautiful—people are beautiful," I sobbed.

"I know," Patty cried. We wrapped our arms around each other, alternately laughing and crying because we were alive. But as we held each other, the raw awareness of death gripped me.

"We wake up every morning, and then what do we do? Then what do we do?" I asked. Patty looked at me blankly, so I rushed on. "Night and day are continuous, not divided. There are no divisions! I mean—people just made up separations that aren't real!"

Patty looked uneasy. "What're you talking about?"

"Life just goes on forever, without any of our reasons or rules. We're in this forever; we can't get out, even when we die! It's a miracle," I concluded.

"You aren't making any sense. You're just stoned," Patty said. "Nobody can figure this stuff out."

"That's what I mean! Why does everyone pretend not to know? I'd even forgotten I was alive! I have to talk to Jim."

"Listen, I'll go get Ray, and he'll talk to you. Then maybe we can go listen to music, OK?"

"OK, for a while." I decided to humor her; she was clearly too worried to be reasonable. As Patty went to get Ray, the idea of seeing Jim calmed me down. We could straighten things out somehow. She returned, hanging on Ray's arm.

"Hi, Judy," he said, smiling down at me. He had a rugged, gentle face, beautifully carved, like the mountains. "Wouldn't you like to get out of your car?"

"You're beautiful," I said. "But I have to go to Hollywood."

"Why don't you get out of the car so we can all go listen to music?"

"We wake up every morning, and then what do we do?" I quizzed him.

"If you get out of the car, we can talk about it."

As I considered this, I noticed some guys in reflector shades and black leather jackets slumped against a wall, snapping gum and staring at us. "Who are they?" I asked nervously.

Ray laughed. "Oh, those guys just take a lot of reds. Don't worry about them. There's nothing to be afraid of."

"I'm not afraid," I said, panicking. "I just have to see Jim."

"You shouldn't drive. There're lots of cops around here." Ray's mellow voice became so grim and authoritarian that I laughed.

"What difference does that make?" I asked, turning on the ignition.

"Ray . . . Judy?" Patty was in tears. I needed to let these nice, over-worried people know we were all alive and free. If no one understood my words, maybe they'd understand my actions.

"We can do anything," I assured them. In one swift motion, I drove my car onto the sidewalk and swept down between the Laundromat and parked motorcycles. At the corner of the pool hall, my steering wheel turned of its own accord, the tires swerved up and down the side-walk; the car had lurched into a life of its own. Careening across the parking lot, it hit a vacant car, jerked back-ward, and mysteriously stalled.

I studied the gearshift knob, choke, clutch, brake, and accelerator with awed confusion. I couldn't remember the right order to start my car; it was way too complicated. Still, it might have been easy enough to leave, my message delivered, if it weren't for the uniformed men gathering around, hissing.

Focused on escaping, I felt a dark force hit me from below. Gripped by a fear of death, I was driven from the land of light, love, and freedom. On this lower plane, it no lon-ger seemed we were created by God but by a scornful machine programmed with repetitive patterns in a calcu-lated cosmic joke. I'd questioned existence too much and violated the consciousness laws, which brought death upon knowledge. My time was running out. Soon my life would ooze away, disintegrate into ectoplasm, only to be remolded. The black and white uniformed men with guns were the official enforcers of the earth laws. Things weren't too subtle on this plane.

"May we have your keys, please?" one of them asked. Stooping over to see my face, he smiled as if he'd made a reasonable request. He seemed gentle and harmless, like he'd taken a crash course in psychology.

"Oh, no, that's OK. I'm just leaving," I said politely. "I can't leave without my keys."

"I don't think you'd better leave right now," he said in a regretful but understanding voice. I bet he got extra points for handling my type.

"It's my car, and I'm leaving."

I gave my keys a violent twist, and the engine came to life. A huge arm reached in, grabbed my keys from the ignition, and unlocked the door.

"They're my keys," I yelled, digging my nails into the arm. "You can't take them. They're mine!" The arm receded, and my car went dead again.

"Will you get out of your car now?" A man with a hooked-beak nose appeared. "We've asked you nicely. Now, are you going to cooperate?"

"No. You stole my keys."

"Get out of the car. That's an order!"

"No!" As I surmised it was their job to capture and kill me, the pit of my stomach tensed into steel wire, waiting to spring. I vaguely recalled it was easier to be calm and not fight death, but I felt too panicked to care.

They huddled around, plotting their next move. A low, hissing noise pressed in on me, black and venomous. A snakelike whip of bodies lashed around my car, and without a word, the men drew in close, forming a tight knot. They broke into my car, pulling and tugging at me. My hands grasped the steering wheel, the gearshift knob, and the seat, but the men dragged me from my car into their territory. As far as I was concerned, this was breaking another earth law. I had the right to fight back.

"You took my keys," I said, attempting to clarify the situation.

"We had to," said the gentle voice. Searching for his face, I was pleasantly surprised to find he looked young and kind. I stared hard into his eyes, and he held the gaze. It passed through time and space; we were playing an absurd game and we both knew it. I hoped we could laugh and explain it to the others. The spell broke instead.

I lunged forward with all my strength, throwing him off balance. After making a few yards of progress, I was seized from behind. I twisted around, lashing at random faces. I swore, kicked, clawed, hit, and bit, breaking away only to be grasped and yanked back again. They weren't going to get me easily; I'd make that clear. But at last, they overpowered me. With two on each side and one behind me, I was literally dragged and thrown into their car.

Handcuffed, I became subdued and disdainful. Having been captured so unfairly, I had no desire to continue living in such a culture. Let them put me to death; I didn't care. As we drove onto the muted gray freeway, the sunset was a diluted brownish-orange, forming a halo of smog above the city.

"Where's Jim?" I asked plaintively.

"Don't start," a matron snapped, glaring at me. I'd interrupted her gossip session with the driver about prisons, job positions, and the new chief. Taxes kept people like me in the back of police cars.

I studied my hands. Long and tapered, they had deep, revealing lines, ancient and wise. I wondered if I knew as much as my palms and turned to see myself in the red lights. My face looked much younger than my hands and not as wise. But underneath, I could detect a basic goodness, and I couldn't imagine why anyone would want to kill me.

I was taken for an interview at a hospital. The attendants made me sit in a wheelchair and restrained me with endless white bandages. After riding a smudged and dirty elevator filled with spooky people, I was wheeled into an iron-barred room where a psychiatrist for law enforcers questioned me. I looked at my driver and backseat matron—they were dying to hear me confess.

"I'll only talk in private," I said.

"All right," the doctor said, shrugging. He then wheeled me into a sterile room with bright lights. From his shrug, I could tell he was weak-willed.

"Will you please take these awful things off me now?" I asked. "I'm not going to do anything."

"I know, but I can't," he sighed.

"Well, can't you even loosen them?"

"OK." He loosened the bandages and turned to me. "Why did you do it?"

"I don't know. Why are you doing this?"

"You mean you don't have any reasons for what you've done?" he asked.

"Why? Should I?" I didn't exactly know what I'd done, but I wouldn't admit that.

"You don't want to talk about it then?"

"There's really nothing to talk about, is there?"

"I guess not." He sighed again, dismayed. "Are you all right?"

I nodded, wanting to confess I was out of my mind, but I thought he should know. He opened the door and pushed me out.

"We're done here. She can leave," he said to my keepers. They looked disappointed.

As they carted me off, I looked back at the man with his humble shrugs and said, "I'm sorry."

Concluding that I'd become a political prisoner, I searched for a possible means of escape. Death no longer seemed the romantic end. Men unwrapped and unloaded me from the wheelchair; then they led me handcuffed across a parking lot. My wrists hurt, and I wondered how they had tied my arms so tight.

"Don't try any funny business," the matron said with surprising foresight. I was deposited in another car. Apparently, they had numerous guest appearances lined up for me. I'd noticed how reliably the colors, textures, and odors of each location reflected the internal dramas taking place. So far, they had been brash colors, dingy textures, grating sounds, and nauseating smells.

In front of a squat gray building, a huge steel plate opened to the sky. We entered, and it slid ominously back down. I was getting sick of this movie and added a little variety to the script when I was questioned next. I changed my last name to Morrison and my age to fifteen and claimed I had no home. This drove the clerks berserk; they asked how many aliases I had (whatever that was, I didn't know). I explained it was all a joke, but they weren't amused.

After more paperwork, I was sent to a waiting room. I sat with a sad walrus type with traffic tickets and a woman with thick black eyeliner, orange hair, and fangs, who'd killed her husband by mistake. They looked me over, and the walrus asked, "What are you doing here?"

"Disturbing the peace, I guess."

"You mean you don't even know what you're doing here?"

"No. I don't fit. I do things in parking lots."

I didn't want to talk anymore, so I rolled into a ball on my bench. Hours later, the officials called my name. It was time for a make-believe bath. Like nurses with daggers in their hearts, they ordered me to undress. Instead of acting embarrassed, I turned it into a long, drawn-out nude scene. One of them caught on to me.

"Hurry up, get it over with," she spit out. "And scrub the tub when you're done."

As soon as I got out of the shallow dish they called a tub, I was sprayed with disinfectant and given a blue prison dress three sizes too big and plastic flip-flops that crippled my walk and made awful noises. I wondered if they had special meetings on how they could degrade women. I was told I could make a phone call but refused to use their telephone.

"But you have to call someone," a large blonde argued. "No one will know where you are!"

"That's fine—I don't either." I glared at her thick belt.

"We'll tell you the address," she said.

"I don't want them to know." Her belt was ridiculous and made her look fat.

"But that's what friends are for—to help you." She was a real philosopher. "What did you do it for?" she half whispered.

"What did I do *what* for?" By now my curiosity was killing me.

"Take LSD. It's a very dangerous drug. You could be dead, you know." She was clearly well informed; my crime was taking acid. "Why did you take it?"

"Because I wanted to."

"Have you done it before?"

"At least forty times. I don't know; I've lost count. It can be interesting." I looked at her and smiled. "You should try it sometime."

This remark was enough for her to report me to the institution's queen. When she came up, the blonde said, "She refuses to make a phone call."

The queen scrutinized me, amazed. "You shouldn't be in a place like this. Why don't you call home?"

"I don't want to." I refused to validate their reality in any way. It was a dream; it couldn't be real.

"It's not too late. You don't have to stay here." She was practically begging. "I'm sure someone will come get you."

"I don't want them to know."

"All right then." She turned angry and cold. "Give me your hands." She took them, rolled them in slimy blue ink, blotted them on paper. "We're going to have to cut off your fingernails now," she warned, getting out her scissors.

"Cut off my fingernails?" I moaned in disbelief. "What's wrong with my fingernails?"

"It's for your own protection. Besides, they're much too long to begin with." She paused sadistically. "If you would just make a phone call, we wouldn't have to do it." I glanced at her crummy, bitten-off nails.

"Go ahead. Cut them off." She wasn't tricking me into any phone calls.

Once my nails were gone, I was escorted down the corridors to my new home. Weird chortling and threatening noises welcomed me. The loud click of the cell door locking was final, but at least I was alone. I lay down on the metal cot. The prisoners were laughing, crying, and singing two-in-the-morning blues songs about their men. They reminded me of Pam crying out, "Sapphire!" I wished everyone would shut up and sleep, but evidently this place ran rampant all night. Somehow, time passed.

⌇

I paced my cell. I hated it—I wanted out. Why hadn't I made a phone call? Did I crash my car? How did I get here?

A bright light flashed in my face, and a surly voice snarled, "Huddleston?"

"I guess," I mumbled disjointedly.

"Your mother's here."

"My mother? Really?" I asked. I couldn't imagine why my mother would be in this place, too.

"Yes, really. You oughta be glad. Come on, I haven't got all night," the voice growled.

I walked through a maze of clothes claiming, hand rolling, clanks, and bars. When I finally reached the prisoner rescue room, my mother was standing alone, looking frantic. I was afraid she'd think I'd turned into one of those legendary LSD vegetables.

"Are you all right?" she asked.

"Look what they did to me," I raged, waving my hands. "They chopped off all my nails just because they

didn't have any. Now they're shaped like squares. Look!"
I held them up to her eyes so she'd get the full impact.

"What happened to your face? You look terrible," she
said.

"I know. I hope it's not permanent."

"Let's get out of here," Mom said. The prison employ-
ees were listening; we gave them dirty looks and walked
out.

Once we were in the car, my mother sighed. "Judy, I
know I can't control you. But if you could just be more
careful from now on. I've never been so worried in my
life!"

"I'm really sorry, Mom." I'd heard her tone of voice
shift. She was liberal to a fault, but I'd gone too far. "I
won't take acid anymore," I promised, hoping it was true.
"I'm never going through that again!" I reached over to
hug her. Our dog, Duffy, nosed in, panting so happily we
both laughed. And we drove off into the night, free, at
least, for the moment.

Catch the Wind

The year 1967 had begun the period of my great alienation. I was light-years away as friends asked me to come to my senses and admit I'd fallen in love with a lunatic who almost made me lose my mind, too. I had a chance to come back, if I'd just forget him—and whatever it was I thought I saw. But their words drifted past, misshapen leaves in the wind. No one knew me or what I'd seen, and I couldn't—and wouldn't—explain. I'd felt close to the core of life: good and evil, love and hate, freedom and bondage. Countless dualities had merged together, but it was too much for me. Overwhelmed, I'd lost everything in fear. I still couldn't let go.

Much of my time was spent alone, reading William Blake, Greek drama, Alan Watts, Dostoyevsky, and comparative religion. I wrote gloomy poems and painted fantasy worlds, but I stopped taking acid. I couldn't piece together what had happened for several months, only remembering vivid but isolated fragments. Years later, I would land in the same mental hospital where I'd been evaluated on acid, the same smudged elevator full of spooky people. After the acid arrest, I tried to retrace my steps, but each took me only further back.

✿

Back in 1966, my boyfriend Bruce and I had dutifully watched *My Fair Lady*; it was already a few years old, but we were clinging to a safe, nostalgic past during that summer before the "real" sixties began. It felt like there was a dramatic split in time, but in truth, the eras simply rolled together and commingled. Sometimes the early to midsixties seemed overlooked, as if the culture somehow sprang full-blown from the Betty Crocker fifties into 1966. It was a jarring leap, and I divided my life before and after 1967—as if I were two people and the first had little relationship to the second.

A few nights after *My Fair Lady*, Bruce and I saw the Lovin' Spoonful at the Golden Bear. "We watched this couple who were completely out on pills," I wrote in my diary. "They were really screwed up!" A folk-rock club in Huntington Beach, the Golden Bear had lots of cool acts: Ritchie Havens, B. B. King, the Butterfield Blues Band. The Lovin' Spoonful sang in a jug-band style that was disconcertingly different from the singles. I was close enough to check out the singer, but I also watched the couple next to us. Probably stoned on downers, they made a sloppy spectacle of themselves, slurring loudly, arguing, and falling together while sloshing drinks across the floor. Not a pretty picture. I would never do drugs, I vowed. Bruce agreed. Unthinkable!

But the child of two alcoholics has certain tendencies. Before summer ended, I decided to stop drinking; there had been incidents. "Wild Thing" had been released and became my anthem as I drank beyond my limits. Tan, blond surfers congregated on patios, beaches, and streets; gallons of cheap red wine flowed steadily; music never stopped. More than a few times I got so drunk I vomited, as if I'd been poisoned. I'd stagger to an empty room and lie down, walls spinning so fast I couldn't move for an hour or two. Eyes shut, I curled up, queasy and cold on some bed, permeated by the sense of being close to people, to the music and laughter of a party, yet stranded on a remote island in the dark. A strangely familiar feeling . . .

I associated drinking with my parents and was determined not to be like them. I primarily stopped due to losing interest in what seemed an inferior, lame activity. I switched addictions as the times caught up with me, and things changed fast. Besides my renunciation of drinking and pull toward art, I'd lost all interest in high school. Within weeks of fall semester, I had rejected it and the years before as absurd. All I cared about was the "real" world—which I comically designated as Hollywood—as far from Newport Beach as possible, a place where I'd find freedom from the archaic past.

Since entering high school, I'd imagined my senior yearbook portrait would be the embodiment of my graduation into the real world. When I scanned the older girls' photos, my favorites had side-parted hair with a grosgrain ribbon, pale lipstick, a sweater, and a single pearl. That look was the epitome of midsixties femininity—the smiling counterpart of the football-wielding, traditional male. But those images had fossilized overnight into the polarized roles embodying straight consciousness. This included me. When we had our senior pictures taken at the beginning of the school year, I wore Bruce's pearl, a sweater, pale smiling lips, and a side-parted long bob. And

I was almost immediately horrified that people might remember me by that retro photo.

I quickly remodeled myself into someone who definitely did not date dumb jocks. The first thing to change was my hair. As notions of masculine and feminine shifted, centering on issues of hair, it's hardly accidental that the times would later be typified by the play of that name. It had to grow out—fast! In the meantime, I could buy a long blonde fall. As we listened to Donovan and smoked joints in her bedroom, Linda and I made collages with pictures from *Look* and *Life* magazine articles about psychedelics, hippies, and Haight-Ashbury. Clearly, most of the hippies in San Francisco didn't have bobbed blonde hair. Instead, it was long and straight, a nondescript brown parted down the middle. The contradictions were growing at a rate I could barely contain.

On our one-year anniversary, Bruce gave me a white-gold ring with a diamond in it. Not long after that, we had our last fight over an *Atlantic Monthly* article I'd given him. "Here," I said, handing him the magazine. "Would you at least read this article?"

"What is it?"

"It's about grass," I said. It was a fair, if liberal, article about the positive aspects of smoking grass. I'd enclosed two joints in a baggie inside the magazine so he could try it without any pressure. I let it go at that, hoping his curiosity would prevail. But when I asked a few days later if he'd read the article, he mumbled, "Most of it."

"What do you mean?"

"If you want to know the truth, it made so mad I couldn't finish it. I threw it away—all of it." He turned his car lights off; we'd just parked outside Mom's.

"You threw the grass away?" That act bordered on unforgivable; when he told me, I went cold inside. "I can't believe you . . ."

"I told you, I don't want to do it." He stared ahead, his chin set. "If you keep going like this, you'll turn into a vegetable."

That was it. I wanted to go into the brave new psychedelic world; he did not. Without another word, I jerked out of the front seat, slammed his car door, and flounced away. He didn't follow me.

෴

Sometime during January, I'd heard the Doors album for the first time. I played it over and over, captivated by the singer's voice . . . that *voice*. I stared at his face on the cover and wondered—it was hard to be sure—if he was "cute." Ah, but just that voice, sounding so eerily familiar, smooth as velvet black around my throat. I was willing to do anything to be with him. I'd been holding myself back for years, waiting for his words to end the lies I'd grown up believing. I rose to embrace the dark side as if it were my deliverance. Much later, I'd find it wasn't the truth; after all the chaotic glory of destruction, I'd feel shocked and betrayed to find that living on the edge wasn't the way, either.

My high-school girlfriend Linda and I visited Bob, who lived on Stone Canyon, across the street from the Hotel Bel-Air, the perfect place to get high around a pool and a rose garden. In his smoke-filled red Camaro, we cruised through the tunneled green canyons of Bel Air. Driving down those lush, winding streets, I wanted the night, the lawns, and the towers to be mine. Sunset Boulevard transformed as we reached Doheny; the neon-lit streets narrowed as the manicured flatlands of Beverly Hills gave way to the tall glass buildings of West Hollywood. This was the new world. After life in the suburbs, the city and its glamour was all I wanted.

Only the west end of Hollywood had the tony landmarks—Scandia and Ciro's—from my parents' days in the music business. We passed Gazzari's at one end of Sunset Strip and the Hullabaloo at another, astonished by the sheer number of kids in vintage clothes, all huddled together smoking joints and laughing as long lines wound into each club's entrance. After our initial tour of the Whisky, the Galaxy, and the Sea Witch, Bob drove us back to his house, and we slept in the Blue Room—utterly unaware of our privileged view as the late sixties were born.

By spring, Linda and I were seeing rock groups every weekend in Hollywood. After a few months, the times I'd felt close to Bruce seemed as distant as another life. Once we'd been melded, hot and liquid, one flesh, and I truly loved him; then he became a barely recognizable stranger from a faraway past.

A Mamas and the Papas song that was popular at the time began, "Strange young girls . . . hiding their madness / Walking the Strip / Soft, sweet, and placid / Offering their youth on the altar of acid." And there were so many of those girls, myself included. We drifted almost aimlessly but with the intent to find the visionary meaning hidden in each moment. As scandalous as the scantily clad dancers under pulsating strobe lights in the Galaxy seemed, what I enjoyed most was crouching over a puddle of oil in a parking lot on the Strip, watching the swirling colors meld as floodlights shifted across the starless sky.

The Kinks, the Yardbirds, the Moody Blues, Procol Harum, Donovan—and, of course, the Rolling Stones— were British imports, but most of the bands we listened to appeared on the Strip: Love, Buffalo Springfield, Iron Butterfly, the Byrds, and the Doors. Even without drugs, it would've been dizzying. Bob's house in Bel Air and the clubs on Sunset Boulevard became our new weekend hangout, a far cry from the hard benches of high school football stadiums. Yet there was a similarity. I was still an enthralled spectator, watching from afar as sweaty but awesome guys performed as if they were gods; near, yet far away, they were like my father singing on TV. It seemed natural that, as before, I'd want to intimately know the players.

One Sunday afternoon that spring, I finally saw him—the singer, the voice—performing at the Cheetah. At the end of a cracked green pier in Venice, the club had been renovated with fake cheetah skins. I wore nondescript clothes—a blue and white pinstriped shirt and faded Levi's—as I stood talking with friends in the lobby. We moved inside the blackened room and sat on the floor.

A spotlight shining through the dark blue silence caught the singer stepping to the microphone. He paused inside the illumined circle; soft light played over his face and held it. He wasn't cute, he was beautiful—and stoned on something I needed, immediately.

I'd been listening to that voice for months, and I wanted to know him, had to know him. I would know him—it flashed through me. After the concert, I saw him walking behind a barefoot, long-haired girl in a miniskirt. Or was she walking behind him? Whatever the order, it looked as if they were on an invisible leash—the way a dog off leash remains attached, aware of the owner's slightest shift. I could sense they belonged together, even though they deliberately walked far apart. In retrospect, this was probably Pam, but the memory is in black and white; I can't see her hair color. It wouldn't have mattered.

Linda and I got in backstage for the first time at the Whisky. "Where there's a will, there's a way," we vowed, standing in a gravel alley behind the club, the damp night black and starry. We were half a block from the gaudy commotion on Sunset, but the moment felt still and hushed as resolution clenched inside me. That saying became our motto as we perfected our psychedelic beach girl method of getting backstage. Contrary to popular belief, to get backstage, nothing was expected beyond a smile.

That night, I finally saw Jim up close, first by the smoky bar, his eyes veiled, an icy drink clinking in his hand, then onstage. He didn't yet seem approachable. I wasn't happy caught in the tight, bobbing crowd, but when he sang "The Crystal Ship," I was spellbound. Then he opened his deliberately closed eyes. Clutching the microphone stand with one hand, he pointed at a white horse flashing across the flowered field of the light-show wall.

The next weekend, we drove to Hollywood again. "Thought we saw Jim," I reported to my diary. "Slept about 2 hrs. Hollywood is groovy. Went to the love-in in Griffith Park at 5 this morning." One of these nights we did see him on Sunset, his arm slung around a long-haired girl as they staggered toward Laurel Canyon. After seeing him stumbling through the neon grove, Linda and I continued on to Canter's on Fairfax, where a nightly line of freaks waited to eat. Then we browsed in a bookstore–head shop. The thinly veiled excitement of discovering a new culture was palpable; we drove back to Sunset to eat chocolate cream pie at Ben Frank's restaurant at 3 AM. Eventually, we parked her blue VW on a quiet side street and slept, curled like shrimp in the small seats, before visiting the love-in at Griffith Park.

At the Hullabaloo in May, Jim appeared like a vision, singular and haunting. As if he'd materialized in a gray time tunnel, he stood at the end of a long empty hall backstage. We walked toward each other for what felt like miles; he aimed his wild, unfocused stare at me. Overcome by his presence, I didn't know what to do but mutely offer him ice from my drink. He ate it directly from my hand and smiled, bleary but sweet. Our eyes met. No words. That was it. He walked on toward the stage. I was hooked, solid. Our first interaction was ice.

A little later that night, I met a girl I'd see often over the next seven months. Denise was the ultimate groupie: tiny, with waist-length brown hair, long bangs, white skin, dark eye makeup, and satin brocade clothes in a gothic hippie look. It was hard to tell if she was pretty or not, her freakiness was so extreme. Nevertheless, she quickly befriended Linda and me, offering us a white lace handkerchief to inhale. Whoa, what was that?

A small, lively redhead danced in and out, holding the liquid stash, which was reportedly Jim's. Either a horse tranquilizer or cleaning fluid (we didn't care), trichloroethane was a clear liquid poured onto cotton or Kleenex and inhaled. The result was an instant, giddy high. But it was short-lived, so frequent doses were required. Sniffing the drenched hankie, a group of us huddled in the shadowed corners of the stage as Jim sang. The performance over, we staggered in alarmed confusion as the entire stage rotated.

Denise may have been with him one night, but more often she wasn't. She'd stand on the sidelines brooding, quiet but friendly, strange—a small, dark, lurking presence. Once she said, somewhat illogically, of Pam, Jim's red-haired main girlfriend, "She must be weird. After all, she's with him." We politely avoided acknowledging that was what we wanted ourselves. I recall thinking that if I were with him, I'd never show up backstage again. Too humiliating, too many girls, too many eyes: at the time, there seemed to be an instantaneous knowing of everyone's thoughts—a kind of fleeting, psychic consciousness.

After the concert, someone claimed the liquid was Energine, a common cleaning fluid. I carried it to school and sniffed it on Kleenex while doodling in class. It's hard to believe that I still went to high school, but I did, inhaling cleaning fluid through civics, which I flunked. I begged, but the teacher wouldn't switch my grade to a D. Passing government was required for US citizens, a status I'd evidently lost interest in. My swan dive from model student to F student was complete. As much as I claimed not to care, this hurt—nearly as much as an earlier homecoming princess disappointment, since I was a "class vamp," proving again I wasn't good enough. For revenge, I got an A the second time. But the damage was done. High school was over.

Breezy, evasive, and flirtatious, Linda and I soon met Ronnie, Rich, and Bill, the band's roadies and future manager, before a concert at an Orange County high school. I can find no record of the concert, but I distinctly recall walking through arched school halls past large shade trees. As the doors came swinging open, light shone through the cracks by the floor; noise rose from inside the auditorium. We found ourselves talking to three guys by an insect-spattered VW bus of sound equipment; they were friendly and familiar, easy to joke with. Bill was the cutest: chestnut brown hair curved around his brow, he had an open smile and seemed the most dutiful. I had the feeling it was his battered blue bus. Rich was the flirtiest, a little on the make. Ronnie, the guitarist's brother, was the cerebral one; turned ironically inward and skewed sideways, he flashed his quirky mind. Since we all hit it off and were about the same age, it seemed natural that when we went to a concert, they'd let us in.

The sense of being possessed, part of an unstoppable current, gripped me; I had to stay close to the source. In July, the backstage security at the Santa Monica Civic Center was so tight that we had to sit in our seats like regular concertgoers. After the concert, Linda peered at me and asked, "Would you really want a guy that wears tight leather pants?"

"What's wrong with that?" I said, shamed by her tone.

"It's just so . . . so sort of Elvis Presley. I mean—it doesn't look like he wears underwear!"

"Well, he's hardly like Elvis," I protested. "He was icky."

Linda's undercurrent of prim scorn summed up our middle-class good-girl upbringing. Surprised she disapproved even as we went to concerts, I felt insulted and confused. Especially by the no underwear comment, which certainly appeared true. But he wasn't all slimy and pathetic, whining like Elvis! Maybe he was kind of weird, like eating mayonnaise with your fingers. My father, whom I rarely saw, would never approve of him or his music. In fact, my father found him worse than Elvis, but censure was the highest recommendation.

Sometimes I traveled faster alone; it was easier to blend in backstage. At the Anaheim Convention Center near Disneyland, I arrived by myself, wearing my long blonde fall. I wore a double-breasted khaki pantsuit, bell-bottoms falling over my stacked boot heels, and a wide suede watchband. Black eyeliner, blush, no lipstick. In the drab, gray dressing room, Jim constructed a wire man from a coat hanger and hung him on the doorframe, adding a wire penis and carefully placing a paper straw wrapper around it. "For protection," he said.

Grace Slick and other members of Jefferson Airplane watched him but did not speak; she left abruptly, without a word, a strange uneasiness trailing behind. Jim seemed loaded on some kind of downer—or maybe just alcohol. Using different intonations, he kept repeating one sentence: "I loves all peoples." The plural sounded both Biblical and incorrect. He was truly peculiar. After the concert, I went along to a nearby restaurant bar, where the service seemed especially slow. When the waiter apologized, Jim shook his head in ironic disbelief. "Excuses, excuses," he drawled across the table. It was barely a whisper everyone strained to hear.

The next day, Linda and I drove to a festival at Devonshire Meadows, a sweltering hellhole somewhere in Northridge. Jim's hair looked strange, too short, blunt, and funny. He wore a puffy white peasant shirt and leather pants. Not only was it daylight, it was unpleasantly hot. I watched from a distance, mildly sickened: too many people, too much smog, too much dirt and dust. Perhaps it was simply too outdoors, too bright for my taste. This time when Jim fell to the stage, the move seemed choreographed. I felt so hot, impatient, and lost in the milling crowd; I just wanted to leave.

In the Cal State L.A. Gymnasium, I was surprised by one of Jim's transparent remarks: he was flattered that a reviewer had said he had a beautiful voice. "He said I had a beautiful voice—no one's ever said beautiful!" I'd imagined he was beyond that kind of thing. Denise stood motionless, as though rooted, furtive and sad as he ignored her. When she smiled, I saw the pain in her dark brown eyes, and it hurt. Wasn't I just like her but acting superior? I'd been wasting my time, months just waiting for him to make a move. I'd usually "gotten" guys this way, but apparently my high-school hard-to-get routine wasn't working on him. His new managers, looking too slick in dark suits, hovered threateningly near, so I kept my distance.

Wearing my black moiré minidress and blonde fall, I walked over to Jim after the concert. "Can I have your autograph?" I asked mockingly, holding out my palm. Without missing a beat, he picked up a stick of incense, asked my name, and scrawled "Judy—Jim" across my outstretched flesh. It hurt a little.

"If I could only just give myself to him . . . I have to be filled up . . . ," I wrote in my diary. So this was what it came down to? This was what finally mattered? My drawings from that time were watercolor, pen and ink, much of the work from dreams. That fall, I started classes at Orange Coast College. I took some required courses but focused on studio art for my portfolio to get into Chouinard Art Institute, a respected fine arts college in L.A. I had no idea of the real art world, but if I hadn't had a discipline to channel my energy, such as it was, I doubt I'd have lived to tell a tale.

All my concertgoing (not that dissimilar to stalking) had built Jim up higher and higher—into the most unattainable god I'd created. God was finally externalized and projected onto one person. Identity, approval, authority, and meaning, all rolled into a single entity. Knowing I was doing this did nothing to stop it—or the years of searching and aiming for him as the solution to my life.

Since childhood, I'd been seeking salvation and comple-
tion through others: parents, teachers, friends, and boys.
But this, this seemed oddly legitimate.

On December 1, the concert was at Long Beach State,
so close that I drove there alone in my pale blue MG.
Driving north on the San Diego Freeway, I drank a half-
pint of vodka straight from the bottle. I wore my short,
forest-green velvet dress and kept the bottle between my
knees; each time I shifted the gears, I felt more determined
that I would really talk to Jim. So far, our exchanges had
consisted of speechless staring and a few sounds.

"I finally made contact," I wrote blissfully. Contact?
Well, perhaps. At one point, Jim brushed up against me
and mumbled something. "Wow," I said—that one syllable
drawn out several beats. That seemed a form of contact.

"I know you're hip," Jim said, as if he was just warming up. But then Pam appeared, all dressed up, and so
cheery she offered me half a stick of her Doublemint gum,
which seemed uncomfortably symbolic. I took it.

A bit later, standing across from me, he looked
bemused and laughed strangely (a startled, low *heh-heh-
heh* sound) as I drunkenly rambled on with Ronnie. Pam
put her hand possessively on Jim's arm and leaned into
him, her long red hair falling in a sheet between us. After
that, my endurance was spent; I headed to the restroom
and threw up. Too drunk to drive, I left my car in the
parking lot and still can't recall how I got home, only
how angry my mother was driving me to retrieve my
abandoned car the next day.

"I just have to be rational and not think about it,"
I wrote in my diary in the morning, trying to counsel

myself. Since the band had two concerts at the Shrine in a few weeks, I could try to forget about Jim until that weekend. Then maybe I'd have a chance to really talk to him, and he would kiss me. And we would fall in love. True love. Just like I always thought it would be. Only there were a few minor problems . . .

Freedom seemed imperative, though I wasn't sure what it meant. To fly from, but also to . . . it was begun with the intent of flying again, as if I'd done it before and merely needed to relearn a rusty skill. Once a friend and I swung as high as we could on her swings, jumping out at the highest point while thinking "lovely thoughts," like Wendy in *Peter Pan*, so we could fly. Fortunately, the grass beneath was thick. Yet we agreed, we'd both felt it—we had flown, if ever so slightly, we had! I'd eat packets of morning glory seeds; sniff Energine cleaning fluid; use alcohol, marijuana, LSD, mushrooms, amphetamines, Valium, cocaine, opium, hashish, and sugar to be free. The morning I ate morning glory seeds and merely vomited them up, I realized I wanted to be crazy, too. The blurring of boundaries had begun. Learning to roll ever more expert joints, I'd thought I still wasn't crazy enough. But now it was 1968; maybe I had succeeded.

Summer in the City

Eventually, late in the spring or early in the summer of 1968, it appeared that I was recovering from my questionable choices. To certify this relative normalcy, I received my official acceptance letter from Chouinard Art Institute in Los Angeles. Everyone was relieved. Art would be my salvation; I could express my imagination and have it accepted as creativity. Linda concluded I had recuperated—my eyes had lost their edgy glint; my sentences were lucid and complete. I was ready for a shopping spree in L.A. for shoes—there were no cool shoes at the beach. So we toured the streets and stores of the city. After finding the shoes old-fashioned, the people unfriendly, and the traffic unbearable, we decided to drop in on Bill, who had become Jim's new manager. We'd always had fun with him and, besides, we had a new marijuana pill called THC to give him.

Before going to Bill's office above the Doors' studio, I asked Linda to circle around the block twice, just to make sure Jim's car wasn't there. It wasn't, but I was gripped by hesitation, so we sat in her parked car. I hadn't seen him since the bad motel scene, about three months before. As little as I'd spoken about the incident, I remained haunted by it.

"If I have to see Jim, I'll die. I'll be so embarrassed—he'll think I'm there for him. I won't know what to say or do or anything."

"His car's not there, so how can he be there? I mean, we can keep checking all day if you want," Linda said. "Besides, I bet you really want him to be there, anyway."

"I do not. You don't really think he's there, do you?"

"No. I already said so." She jiggled her keys impatiently.

"Well, he better not be. If he is, I'll just ignore him. I can't stand him anymore."

"'I can't stand him,'" Linda said, imitating me. "Sure. That's why you keep talking about why he's there or not and what you'll do and—"

"Oh, shut up. I'll go," I said, and got out of the car. I had never explained what really happened when I last saw him, and I was not about to now.

We arrived in our typical slapstick style. Bill was sweet, saying we were the same old comedy team. He had to step out to make a phone call, so we sat down and waited. I picked up a notebook from the table beside me—a chaotic collection of Dada-esque poems illustrated with squashed tubes of toothpaste, soup cans, bananas, and trash cans. I wasn't sure if the creator had seen too much or too little Andy Warhol. When Bill came back, he told us the book was just left for Jim. "He's always getting these things from people, wanting his opinion." I almost felt sorry for Jim.

Bill joked with us a while; we talked about a few friends. Then he said they were having a short business meeting but to wait around. I wanted to stay, but I also wanted to go. Since I was already there, it seemed I should stick it out. I compromised by sitting under a huge rubber plant by the door. Since it was the same shade of green as my clothes, I imagined I blended in, subtly camouflaged. Linda had quickly befriended the secretary of the moment and was giggling in the corner with her. I felt safe and inconspicuous as someone thudded up the stairs. It was Ray Manzarek, the organist, who recognized me as an old backstage remnant and smiled. "Oh, I see we have some new scenery. . . . I was getting tired of that plant anyway. This is much better." He was obviously aware that I thought I was a plant. That unnerved me, but it was too late.

Then two more band members trudged through the door and didn't notice me, so maybe it was good camouflage. Slow, deliberate footsteps climbed the staircase—I knew they belonged to Jim. There was nowhere to run or hide. But maybe he'd be too preoccupied to notice. A petrified statue, I looked straight ahead while his face came into view. The same face, the same husky voice said, "Hello."

I cracked out a noise of recognition, and he strode into the business meeting. As the band talked and Linda continued giggling, I wondered why the hell I'd gotten myself in this situation. Soon Bill came out and walked us downstairs. Linda and I followed him to the parking lot as he apologized about his lack of time and thanked us for the THC. Girls and roadies were coming and going; trucks, cars, and sound equipment crowded the lot. Jim descended the staircase, taking it all in with a bored look. He nonchalantly inspected a motorcycle and then walked over to me.

"Can you give me a ride?" he asked. "It's just to Westwood."

"I don't know; it's not my car. My friend is driving." I was supposed to be mad at him but had frozen in panic.

Jim turned directly to Linda, who looked confused by my bad manners. "May I have a ride to Westwood?" he asked her.

"Sure." Linda smiled warmly, making up for my icy attitude. Jim's hair had been cut, and he looked sort of stupid.

"You cut your hair. What did you cut your hair for?" I blurted out. "I liked it better before, when you looked like a lion."

"I know," he said, showing no humility about his previous lion look. "But it was getting so long—I couldn't even wash it right. I don't trust people with my hair, but I was told this guy was good. Now it's too short! I don't care." He shrugged.

Jim sat in the backseat after a flurry of deciding who should sit where. Tongue-tied, I felt he'd changed from a lion into a demented chipmunk. I remembered Pam also bore a vivid likeness to a chipmunk. They must be meant for one another, after all, I thought. In no way could my face be construed as having chipmunk features. What a way to realize we weren't soul mates.

"How long have you two been friends?" Jim asked, sounding like a refined old gentleman on a transatlantic cruiser.

"I can't remember," I said, glancing at Linda who was busy not crashing into the curb. "I guess about five years."

"That's a pretty long time," Jim said, his voice full of high regard. He looked at Linda in her rearview mirror as she turned red and confused. "You even look like sisters," he added. We were both tan with blonde hair and light eyes, like about a million other California girls. Jim kept staring at Linda, and she turned even redder.

"Just look at that!" I said, pointing at a poodle trotting along the sidewalk. "All clipped and bowed and manicured. . . . God, I can't stand poodles!" I added, knowing Linda couldn't either and might speak up.

"Are you moving to Silver Lake when you start Chouinard?" Jim asked, ignoring my poodle tirade.

"I don't know yet. . . . It's not until September." I'd never even heard of Silver Lake.

"I used to know a girl who lived there," he said remorsefully, as if she was dead or something. I felt a twinge of jealousy for the sadly fleeting girl. "You know this album we're working on now?" Jim's voice rose louder, and I turned. "Well, I think it's the best we've ever done! I know everyone says that about what they're just finishing, but I still think it is."

"That's good. Maybe it is the best. What are you going to call it?" I asked, wondering if Linda had lost her capacity for speech.

"I think the title will be *Waiting for the Sun*. It's *Waiting for the S-u-n*, not *S-o-n*." He wrinkled his face quizzically, seeming to find this point significant.

"Yeah, that makes more sense," I said, and his worried face relaxed.

Jim directed us down a side street in Westwood lined with shoe repair shops, old drugstores, and dental offices. He asked us to stop in front of one of the gray buildings. "Would you wait for me while I run upstairs and make sure my friend is there?" he asked. "I'll come right back down." He had a way of turning questions into statements. Linda nodded; I smiled. Jim bolted out the door and up the stairs.

"I wish I could sneak up and see what his friend is," I whispered to Linda. He gave the word such mysterious meaning—male, female, somewhere in between?

"Judy, you don't have to whisper; he can't hear us," Linda practically yelled. Then she smirked. "Gee, Jim Morrison was sitting in the backseat of my car. What do you think I should do?"

"Polish it, put up a DO NOT TOUCH sign. And don't let anyone sit there, ever."

"Maybe I can make some money," she joked.

"Do you think he has a new breed of person in there, or what?" I asked. We lapsed into giggles and were verging on hysterics when he approached.

We calmed down, sedate little soldiers. Linda muttered, "I like these pants better than the black ones." My face twisted with held-in laughter as Jim assured us his friend was home, so he wasn't stranded. He thanked Linda so profusely for the ride that one would think she'd donated her last drop of blood. Then he leaned over and practically pulled me out of the car.

"Call me tomorrow and give me your phone number. I've got to see you again," he whispered.

I couldn't understand the need for such an elaborate procedure when I could just write down my number, and I wasn't sure why he was whispering like it was a big secret. I looked at him uncertainly. It must have been the drama.

"I'll answer the phone, don't worry," he rushed on. "Just be sure and call at one thirty, all right?"

"OK, I will," I said.

"Don't forget!" He used his everyday voice—so deep, so sure. I was hooked again.

〜

I called on time. A male voice answered, but I didn't want to be presumptuous.

"May I speak to Jim, please?" I asked, astounded by my steady voice.

"This is Jim." He sounded slightly offended. I was touched that he had really answered the phone at one thirty. He didn't seem the telephone-answering type.

"Oh, good. It's Judy."

"So . . . you called."

"Yeah."

"I've been wanting to see you again for a long time," he said. "You just disappeared!"

I silently wondered what else I could have done. Jim used the telephone as an extended microphone, imbuing it with the same caressing seduction. You became the most important, desirable person alive.

"What are you wearing?" he asked.

"My bathing suit and a top."

"What are you doing?" he asked. I got the feeling he hoped I was at an orgy, barely able to speak between gasps.

"I'm sitting on the floor, getting ready to go to the beach." I was so boringly honest that I should have added I was barefoot and cross-legged.

"That must be nice," he replied wistfully. "I'm going to Hawaii for ten days. I want to learn to surf in between performances." I couldn't imagine his pale, delicate body converting into a brawny, brown surfer's, and I nearly laughed.

"Well, have a good time there," I said, wondering why I had to call if he was just leaving town again.

"Now, what's your phone number?" he asked. I recited it. "Be a good girl while I'm gone."

"I will."

"I'll call you as soon as I'm back." That sounded a bit familiar, but I agreed, shaken by the unspoken promise I heard in his voice. We hung up the phone.

My Eyes Have Seen You

Around five in the morning, the phone rang, breaking dawn's quiet reign. "Judy, it's for you," my mother called groggily. I staggered half-awake into the living room and picked up the receiver.

"Hullo . . ."

"Hi—it's Jim!" He sounded like a bright child answering an impossible algebra problem. I actually didn't recognize his voice.

"Jim who?" I asked.

"Jim!" The persistent, plaintive cry came through. "Don't you even remember me?"

"Oh, yeah, I remember you," I answered. I'd hardly forgotten; it had been about a month since I saw him at the office in L.A. My heart beat wildly; I felt faint.

"You don't sound very glad to hear from me."

"I am. It's just that I was asleep."

"You gave me the wrong phone number! All I got was a gas station in Culver City. What did you do that for? Then I had to go ask Ronnie for it, and he didn't even know what it was! So I called information. There was only one Huddleston in Corona del Mar, so I figured it had to be you." Jim sounded proud of suffering through such an ordeal. "Why did you give me the wrong number?" he asked.

"I didn't do it on purpose," I said. "You must've forgotten to use the area code. There's a different one down here." It seemed like he should be able to figure this stuff out.

"Why didn't you tell me then? Will you come up and see me?" he asked in a woebegone voice.

"When?" I asked.

"Now."

"Now? Well, um, where are you?"

"Hollywood," he said, like where the hell else would he be?

"Yeah, well, where in Hollywood?" I asked.

He named the Beverly Terrace Hotel, corner of Doheny and Melrose, suite number, and floor.

"Are you going to come?"

"Yes. But I'm an hour away, you know." I felt sure he hadn't the faintest idea where Corona del Mar was. My mom came into the room, shook her head, and rolled her eyes.

"But will you leave right now?"

"Well, I have to put on some clothes first," I stalled.

"How long will that take?" he asked sarcastically.

"About ten minutes, I guess."

"And then you'll leave? Are you really coming? Promise me you're coming."

"I promise. I'm coming," I repeated to my mother's smothered laughter.

"Please hurry!" he pled as if he was dying. Then he hung up.

My hair looked like hay-colored seaweed, frizzy from too much sun and saltwater, and all my clothes seemed ugly. I put on some mascara, stuck rollers in my hair, and hoped I wasn't too tan for him. Rushing around in a frenzy, I selected some clingy brown clothes and reasoned I'd look all right when I got there. I finally stopped to say good-bye to my mother.

"I just have to go," I told her.

"I know, honey." Mom shook her head. She looked up at the ceiling in mock nausea and sighed. "Just don't crash your car hurrying. I'm sure he can wait."

"Do you think I'm being stupid?" I asked.

"Would it make any difference? You'd do it anyway," she replied, summing up my stubborn irrationality. "I just wouldn't take him too seriously, honey." That roused my defenses; I wanted to explain that my eyes were wide open. But she smiled; she knew. I still wished she wouldn't assume the worst about him, but she waved me off before I could argue about Jim's integrity.

I drove with the dawn, racing to beat the rush hour behind me. Just as the San Diego Freeway met the Harbor Freeway in another smog-town named Carson, my car died with four long, drawn-out chugs. I yanked the rollers out of my hair, pulled on the boots I couldn't drive in, and jumped onto the side of the freeway. Before I had to pose as a helpless female betrayed by her classically worthless car, a farmer in a red truck stopped for me.

"I can only take you as far as the airport. Will that help?" The man had a pleasantly weathered country face and spoke in a slow, twangy drawl, smiling encouragingly.

"Yes, thank you," I said, scrambling into his truck.

"No use rushing, we won't get there any faster," he observed, indicating the deluge of traffic with an amused nod. This man was so perfectly incongruous and cheerful, I relaxed into peaceful silence. Everything was fine, after all. He didn't even ask why I was simply abandoning my car like a dead relay horse.

When he dropped me at the airport intersection, I plunged into the street, practically killing myself to make a taxi stop. The driver had uneven spots of gray hair and a sneer-etched, skinny face. When I asked to go to Hollywood, he turned around, brusquely sizing me up. "I don't mean to be offensive, but do you have the money?" he asked.

"Is fifty dollars enough? I mean, if you take the direct route?" I added. "Would you like to see my wallet?"

"No. It's just that you never know anymore," he grumbled.

I pulled out brown eye shadow and lip gloss to finalize my appearance. When we stopped in front of the hotel, I overpaid my fare, hoping this would teach the man not to underestimate girls. Inside, the concierge sat like a sophisticated watchdog by the front desk. He stared at my breasts; then he tried my eyes. I gave him a blasé look and walked purposefully up the stairs.

Finding the right room number, I knocked softly on the door. No response. I began knocking loudly and softly calling, "Jim?" Still no answer. Not only was my car abandoned on a freeway, I was stranded in a strange hotel corridor, hissing at a door. Tired of being subtle, I yelled his name and banged on the door. He finally appeared, half-drunk or half-asleep, and totally naked.

"Oh, you're here," he said, letting me in. Rubbing his eyes and yawning, he walked in confused semicircles before stumbling off for a glass of water.

I stood by the door, watching him. He didn't seem very appreciative. Though hurt by his careless attitude,

I was distracted by his appearance. He had a truly beautiful body, shaped like classical Greek sculpture; it was perfect, without overstated lumps and bulges. It seemed like a male equivalent of mine, not threatening or alien. Revived by the water, Jim sauntered around, posing provocatively, and then sat down on the bed.

"What took you so long? It's been hours! I gave up hope," he said.

"My car broke down."

"Oh, why didn't you tell me?" he asked. He patted the bed beside him. I stared at him hesitantly. Lying down on his side, he half smiled up at me. "Aren't you taking your clothes off?"

I felt pretty stupid standing there, all dressed up, expecting a proclamation of love—or at least more ardent lust. After my car fiasco, some expression of desire would have helped. I pulled off my top as slowly as possible, prolonging the process of stripping myself bare without promises. I wasn't wearing a bra, so there wasn't the suspense of removing several layers of clothes. Only three meager items to shed, and it was instant skin. Jim didn't seem disappointed. He pulled me down next to him without hesitation. I wanted to rebel but remained silent, letting myself roll aimlessly on the bed with him. It was sort of fun, actually, frolicking like clumsy puppies. When he kissed me, the purpose was clear, transfusing me with warmth.

"Eat me," he said in a long, sensual drawl, causing an electric bolt of shock and excitement to shoot through me. I felt strangely, totally alive.

Life was fluid; I eased into the mood shift through skin on skin. We went a little deeper.

"Why did you give me the wrong phone number?" he asked once he was inside me.

"I didn't. I told you—I forgot the area code."

"And I got a gas station. A gas station! You did it on purpose. You wanted me to go through this, to hunt all over to get your number. Didn't you?" I watched him silently, wishing I could have done something like that. "Then you didn't even remember who I was." His voice sounded hurt, outraged, and thrilled.

"I was asleep. It was only five in the morning."

"You bitch—you did it on purpose! You really are a bitch, aren't you? Answer me!"

But I didn't. I couldn't. I'd ruin the wonderfully ruthless character he had invented for me and bore him with my wholesomeness.

"How many men have you fucked since me?"

"None," I said, wishing I knew something better than the truth. Embarrassed, I looked away. I was so hung up on him that other guys seemed tame, dumb, and vastly inferior. But I'd never admit that.

"How many?" he demanded. "I won't get mad. I just want to know."

"None," I repeated, forcing myself to meet his eyes. He looked at me with open disbelief. Both relieved and disappointed, I wanted to laugh, so I bit my lip.

"You're lying." Jim carefully watched my face. "Aren't you?"

"No. Really, it's the truth. No one," I said, feeling my eyes begin to flicker. It was so funny that he wouldn't believe the truth. I had to think of something sad to make my eyes stop laughing.

"Are you making fun of me?" he asked. I shook my head, distrusting speech. "You're a bitch and a whore, a bitch and a whore! And you love it . . ."

Too shy to protest, I adapted to my wicked new role instead. Then the mood changed, became airy and flowing; we were on an aimless pleasure ride. The early morning sun filtered softly through the French windows, gently illuminating us. Insulated from the outside world, we moved slowly in front of the gilded mirror. We looked lovely, our striking contrasts molded together in warm, rich patches of light from a pre-Raphaelite painting. My tawny masses of red-gold hair fell over his translucent white skin. Soft black waves framing his pale face, Jim's blue eyes shot steadily through the mirror, pinning me there, locking us in time.

"We're animals fucking," he said, moving behind me. "You're an animal." I felt an almost predatory quality in my own carnality and something ethereal and feminine emanating from his dark frailty. "We're wild dogs, fucking," Jim insisted, holding me to him. I felt frightened by the fiery vitality, the voluptuous presence that threatened to take over the mirror and overpower us. I was relieved when we tumbled back down on the bed.

"Remember that time I fucked you in the ass?" He gave it a sweet lilt, as if reflecting on a walk in the summer rain.

"Yes." I would've forgotten it if I could.

"Don't you want to do it again?" he asked, moving slow and soft.

"I told you I didn't like it the first time."

"But I'll be very gentle," he pled.

"No, I don't want to!"

The door to the room opened and then quickly closed. Jim lost control of himself in an erratic climax. I felt pleased, in a vehemently illogical way.

"It was the maid," Jim said. He fixed his pillow so he could lean sideways and look at me. "I didn't feel like coming, you know. I just wanted to enjoy it. Then she walked in . . . I wasn't expecting that! I wonder why it affected me that way?" His eyes filled with wonder—and a child's wild hope that I could explain his behavior.

"I don't know," I answered. I didn't know why he did anything, but I gathered that analyzing behavior was one of his hobbies.

"You know I don't really think you're a whore, don't you?"

"Yeah," I said.

"You mean you understand?" he sounded elated.

"I think so," I said gloomily. If I was as fickle and free as he was, I'd be more exciting, and he wouldn't have to worry about hurting me. I couldn't let him know I was secretly faithful and, worst of all, believed he'd eventually fall in love with me.

Jim stood up cheerfully, saying he had to make some business calls. He placed his hand on my head, gently rubbing it as he dialed. He used his intimate public voice, still sexy and husky but more refined and gracious, deepened with authority.

"Hey, listen, this is serious. My hotel bill better be paid right away, or they might throw me out on the street. And they won't take anyone's check." Placing one hand over the receiver, Jim put his other hand under my chin, lifting my face so he could see it better. "You're beautiful," he said.

I smiled, thinking it was about time he'd noticed. Now maybe he'd see I was an unusual human being, too. He hung up the phone and started dressing.

"I've got to meet everyone downtown for passport pictures and some other hassles. It'll be hot and smoggy, but you can rest here. I won't be gone more than a couple hours at the most. Won't you stay?"

"Yes." I was certainly in no hurry with my car lost somewhere on the 405 freeway.

"Good. Then we can make love some more. You'll really be here when I come back?"

"Yes," I said, giving him a small smile.

"See you soon, then," Jim said. Then he locked me in his room.

Relieved to be alone, I felt devious enough to look through the drawers. Instant karma lashed out in the form of a note on U-Haul paper. "Jim, I'm off for England. Hurry over. I love you. Pam."

I studied her words and writing for about three minutes. Then I slammed the drawer shut. Pam's handwriting looked just like her; it was if I could hear her lilting voice. Walking wearily to the bathroom, I hoped a good hot shower would help.

Stepping into the shower stall, my eyes closed like a supplicant. I hoped the hot water cascading down my body would restore me. Through a filter of steam, I watched drops of water form on the creamy ivory tiles, fall together, and slide down in glistening trails. Leaning against the cool wall, I looked down at a blood-stained bikini bottom lying on the turquoise blue tiles. This was almost more sickening than Pam's note. As rivulets of water eddied down the silver drain, I wondered where the owner had left her top and what happened to her. Weakened, I got out of the shower.

Wrapped in a Turkish towel, I left the bathroom and turned on the Democratic Convention. I walked around the room, letting the air dry me off. My eyes fell upon a pair of pantyhose hanging forlornly on the window ledge; the toes were gently draped over the back of a lemon brocade chair. This was just too much evidence to digest. I was nauseous. My towel fell to the floor, and I collapsed across the bed. I felt too sick to cry.

Jim's lyrics whirled through my brain: "I dwelt in the loose palace of exile / Playing strange games with the girls of the island." I'm not some dumb island girl, I thought, shivering and cold. Curling into a fetal position, I pulled the covers over my head. I fell into something like sleep. Eventually, it was impossible to breathe, and I rationalized that he had some reason for doing these things. I threw off the covers and came out of hiding.

Greeted by my mirrored image, so fresh and healthy, I couldn't imagine why he wasn't in love with me. With my long bangs and hair redder from the sun, I could even see a little of Pam's chipmunk look. Just from some angles, though—my cheekbones were too high, and my nose wasn't short enough. Still, I felt confident again, brushed my hair, and turned up the TV. They were saying all sorts of amusing things at the political convention. I felt fine when I heard Jim's whistling coming down the hall. For someone who was supposed to be so tragic, he sure whistled a lot. Then he opened the door and smiled, as if he'd just come home.

Season of the Witch

Jim seemed happy, full of animated talk about the great Japanese restaurant they'd found downtown.

"Oh, I shouldn't be talking about food; you're probably hungry. Are you? We can eat somewhere if you are," he said.

"No, I'm not at all, really." This was true. Food sounded repulsive.

"Have you been bored?" he asked, assured I wasn't hungry.

"Actually, it's been nice doing nothing for a change. It's kind of relaxing."

"Yeah, it is good for you," Jim agreed, lying down beside me and smiling sweetly. He sighed and rolled his head across the pillow to look up at me shyly, almost worshipfully. His eyes were wide and vulnerable, with a boy's do-you-like-me look. When he took his defenses away like that, it blew me away. All I wanted to do was reassure him, love him; he was a stray child with no mother, lost in the world. We felt raw and tender in the moment and held each other with all the love we'd never found. It seemed the warmth and strength of those who will forever be friends.

"If it wasn't for this, life wouldn't be worthwhile," Jim said, his voice near tears.

The desolation in his words scared me, but then he transformed like a desert storm. He wanted to make love and threw off his clothes as his desperation mounted. "Now. Now. Now," he cried over and over. I knew he wanted to feel the moment, but it seemed like he was onstage and I was watching from a distance.

"What are you?" he asked.

"I don't know." I looked at him in confusion. "A girl?"

"No. You're a cunt," he said, with the uninflected patient tone of a teacher speaking to a possibly gifted student. His pupils dilated, forming a black core that penetrated me. I felt his violence prickling under my skin, threatening to erupt between us. "Now, what are you?"

"A cunt."

"Whose cunt?"

"Mine, my own," I blundered defiantly.

"No! You're mine. You're my cunt." He gave me a desperate, searching look; his voice was raw. "Do you understand that? You're only mine. I own you." He scrutinized me, waiting for resistance. I gave none, feeling strangely secure and comforted, as if we were locked together in some primal way. His harshness subsided.

"Now, what are you?"

"A cunt."

"Whose? Say it."

"I'm yours. I'm your cunt."

Later, lying peacefully entwined, Jim asked, "Do you know what I mean when I talk to you like that?"

"I think so," I said. I felt he was trying to define sexuality, reducing us to the basic elements.

"It's hard to explain," he began.

"No. I do know what you mean," I said. And I thought I did.

"You know, we really get along well, don't you think?" he asked, an astonished look spreading across his face. "We should spend a lot more time together. It's so easy to be with you!"

"It's easy to be with you, too," I smiled, thinking he was pretty slow to catch on. We just stared at each other, embarrassed.

"How old are you now?"

"Eighteen."

"You're pretty young," Jim said doubtfully.

"I'll be nineteen later in August," I answered.

"You take birth control pills or something, don't you? I mean, if we're going to keep seeing each other, we don't want you getting knocked up or anything."

"I grew up on them," I said icily. I hadn't heard that expression since I first started taking pills. I wondered how many girls he'd knocked up so far. "I'm hungry now," I announced. It was getting dark outside, and I hadn't eaten breakfast before I left in the morning.

"Uh, there's a little problem. I forgot, but there's a friend coming to meet me for dinner. I guess we can all go together." He looked confused. "I'm afraid all three of us would be awkward?" Besides his ability to turn questions into statements, he was deft at making statements questions.

"I don't see why it has to be awkward. Besides, I'm starving to death and sick of being inside."

"I guess you're right, after all." Jim smiled, easily convinced. "Let's get dressed now, so we won't be late. I'm always late!"

When we walked outside, the smog in L.A.'s air had produced a twilight mirage of color; the evening sky glowed an incandescent lavender, pink, and salmon. Between hibiscus and oleander, Jim's friend stood barely illuminated under the palms.

"You look like you're hiding," Jim joked.

"Shouldn't I be?" A guy with a dark beard and intelligent face laughed. When we were introduced, he was friendly, but he forgot my name twice on the way to his car. By the time he said he remembered faces, not names, I felt too embarrassed to admit I hadn't caught his name, either. Piled into his tiny convertible, we drove down Sunset Boulevard. The night was warm, the lights sparkling; the wind felt good in my hair.

"I don't like to talk shop, but . . . ," Jim said, going on about how much his record was grossing. His friend discussed some great new equipment that was too expensive but that he planned to use on his next film anyway. Jim threw me a strange look, maybe because I wasn't talking.

"The lights are pretty," I said.

"I know. See, this is why I like the city. It's good neon." When we'd had a debate over the good and bad points of L.A., I'd said it was too flashy. He seemed pleased to have proven his "good neon" point without even trying.

We entered a small Hungarian restaurant named Drossi's, with red-checked tablecloths and an intimate atmosphere. Jim apologized about the too-warm wine and then smirked. "I hear you're quite a drinker," he said.

"I used to drink a lot," I said. Flushing crimson, I hoped he wasn't referring to the time I got drunk backstage on vodka, wine, and Scotch. That night at the Long Beach State concert, he'd whispered that he knew I was hip and slipped me Scotch when Pam wasn't looking. I'd gotten sick in the restroom but didn't think he knew. My mind careened to the time I fed him ice cubes in a hallway and back to the gypsy card reader in the corner. "Once I had my handwriting analyzed on Olvera Street. She told me I was going to be a veterinarian when I grew up," I said.

"Really? Do you even like animals?" the filmmaker asked.

"Actually, I like them a lot. But I paint." I noticed the awful paintings hanging on the walls. "Not this kind of painting."

"I guess you won't be painting animals, then." He laughed and launched into his disillusioning meeting with Herbert Marcuse, who was wearing a stupid button. I had no idea what Marcuse had to do with gypsies; he apparently possessed an influential mind, though he was an inhospitable creep in person. I laughed and listened but felt disconnected. Jim pressed my knee under the table, and I met his indefinably sad gaze.

"You know, I've always wanted to do a really good death scene," Jim said. "It would be in a meadow under some trees." The waiter arrived with dinner and began serving. "And there'll be blood on the white flowers falling over my face," he continued.

"The beef stroganoff," the waiter said, clearly not amused.

"Oh, excuse me," Jim said, choking in mock horror. "You shouldn't talk about death at the dinner table!" The waiter left haughtily as I discreetly gulped more wine and Jim collapsed into adolescent laughter. The bearded man began a diatribe on film and theater criticism.

In the middle of enjoying my beef stroganoff, I looked up, stricken. "I'm eating meat. If vegetarians weren't so preachy, I'd probably stop. I keep eating it on purpose, they make me so mad!"

"I think it's a new form of religion." Jim sounded both amused and respectful. He segued to his upcoming trip to Europe, but I was still feeling guilty about the slaughtered animals. In England, he hoped to meet the Beatles, although he was afraid they'd never heard of him, or, if they had, that they'd reject him.

"Couldn't you have tea with them? They have tea for everyone, don't they?" asked the filmmaker. He then answered himself: "Yes, it's their custom, at three in the afternoon or something."

"What if they just laugh at me?" Jim asked.

"I think you should just do it," I said, tired of all the fuss.

Jim looked slightly offended. He turned to the subject of Mick Jagger, whom he'd seen backstage, though they didn't speak. This seemed to prove English rock stars hated him. "Jagger looked like he'd been through a lot of hard times but came out all right." That sounded like a statement to the press, and I wished there was more warm wine.

The filmmaker said it'd be interesting to see how *Hair* was done in L.A. after New York, adding we'd better leave or be late. I didn't know where we were going, but on the way there, Jim told a story.

"When I was young, my mother watched Art Linkletter on TV every day. She was really hung up on him. One day, he said he was a passionate collector of those baseball cards that came with bubblegum, you know? So, my mother, she believes him; she goes out and buys all this gum and mails him all the cards. I don't know what she thought would happen!" He laughed. "Then a few weeks later, Art told the audience he'd just been putting them on. My mother was heartbroken. That's when I decided I had to get into the entertainment business."

We all laughed. I didn't know if this was true or something he'd just invented. As we pulled up in front of the Huntington Hartford Theater, Jim leapt out without warning. "I'll buy the tickets now, so we don't have to stand in line," he called, darting into the crowd. As we parked the car, the filmmaker was still laughing.

"Jim's really funny," he said.

"Yeah, he is. I have a headache, though. Do you have an Excedrin?" I rubbed my temples.

"No, I'm sorry, I don't have any aspirin." He sounded sympathetic and had nice brown eyes, so I revealed my cure for headaches.

"If I just concentrate on not thinking, it'll go away," I said.

"But you can never stop thinking!" He sounded so dogmatic that I stopped rubbing my temples. I was planning a retort about monks in caves when Jim found the car. Looking exhilarated, he handed us tickets as if each had a secret meaning. The night looked jewel-lit down Vine as he led us through the crowds into the theater.

Called *Do Your Thing*, the play featured people cavorting about, spouting happy and free lines about being androgynous and doing their own thing. I hoped it was really satire. Jim was concerned that one of the actresses had her zipper open. Maybe he ought to go pull her fly up, or at least tell someone? But he didn't, in case it was intentional. He mumbled about how backward and uncomfortable he felt in an audience.

When the play ended, I was relieved to find they were disappointed. But when Jim didn't hold my hand or put his arm around me—didn't even jab me in the ribs—I picked apart my appearance piece by piece for the reason. By the time we were back in the car, heading for another unknown destination, I was sulking. I just wanted to be in bed with him, even if he was crazy. I wanted him to be mine like he said I was his.

Minutes later, we were sitting in the Los Feliz movie theater watching French shorts about adolescence and sex. They were good; they felt real. The main feature flashed by in a series of images. After a brutal war scene, a group of soldiers terrorized a small country family. They held a gun up a woman's skirt to prove their masculinity; then they hunted down and shot an anarchist Joan of Arc–type woman like a deer in the woods.

Jim left for a Coke and, when he returned, growled in my ear. "Fancy meeting you here. Haven't we met before?" The soldiers were back home showing off picture postcards of Athens, Rome, and Paris, bragging of their conquests in the midst of their impotence. The movie was good but depressed me so much I didn't want to talk.

When we walked outside, the night seemed almost scandalously beautiful, the full moon shrouded by ragged clouds. Jim and his friend rattled on, oblivious. Surprisingly, the filmmaker turned to me and asked my opinion on the postcard scene.

"Oh, she's fallen asleep already," Jim said.

"I have not!" I protested. "I found it alternately fascinating and boring—back and forth."

"That is a problem Godard has with repetition," the filmmaker agreed. "Sometimes he pushes it too far. It's a tricky technique to use right."

I was glad he thought I was intelligent and hoped Jim saw that, but they lapsed back into analyzing film devices. I contemplated staging a bloody, wordless suicide on the corner of Highland and Sunset as an alternative technique, but I'd probably just end up with a broken arm.

At the hotel, Jim's friend, evidently having forgotten our headache-and-thinking clash, asked if I'd like a ride. He'd obviously observed the muted rapport Jim and I were sharing. Surrounded by silence, Jim pulled a poker face. I should have left before things went from bad to worse.

"No. Thanks, anyway," I said.

Jim and I got out of the car and walked inside.

My boots sounded too noisy, squeaking terribly as we climbed the stairs. Inside his room, I admitted the truth.

"I don't know where my car is. I left it on a freeway somewhere. I just left it there!"

"I do things like that, too. Sometimes you just feel like it . . ." He paused. "Shouldn't you call someone and tell them where you are?"

"I guess."

"Feel free to call anywhere you want. The phone's right there." He motioned in case I was blind, and tromped off to the bathroom.

"I'm not dead, in case you were wondering," I said to my mom, hoping she'd understand my fake frivolity. She did, and she then began a series of what's-he-doing questions. I came up with a lot of cryptic sentences, letting her know I was OK but the situation was bad. As soon as I hung up, Jim came out, toothbrush still in hand, and stared at me.

"You must be awfully close to your mother to talk to her like that."

"Yeah, I am," I said. At that point, it seemed too complicated to explain our atypical relationship.

He'd had the nerve to put on a ridiculous pair of boxer shorts, as if to protect himself from me. When he slid into his side of the bed, I kept sitting there, fully clothed, wondering what to do. My car was stranded, it was late, I'd refused the ride I should've taken, and I was too embarrassed to call my friends.

"Well, what are you doing?" Jim finally asked.

"Thinking."

"Are you getting in bed, or what?"

I couldn't think of anything else to do. I undressed, making sure my bikini underwear shielded me. He'd better know I wasn't in the least interested in him, either. I moved to the far right side of the bed, so near the edge I was about to fall on the floor. I turned over on my side with a belligerent movement and glared at the dark wall. I'd never felt so rejected, so unloved. I hated him.

"Have you ever had a boyfriend?" he asked. I couldn't have dreamed a worse insult.

"One and a half," I replied sarcastically. Then, to my horror, I explained the answer honestly. "I mean, I've had a lot of minor boyfriends, but only one and a half major ones."

"Oh, it's all just impossible," Jim said in a stunned, tragic voice. "It never works out. Something's always wrong. You believe all these things about love, but it's never true the way you thought. Still, you keep believing something will work, but it's just not possible!"

"What about Pam?" I asked, cast into this role of sharing love's hopelessness. I'd always felt she was what kept me from him. I wished he'd just come out and stab me with his devotion to her.

"Pam?" he questioned the name vaguely. "Oh, I don't know—she doesn't really understand me. . . . We've been together off and on for a few years. It's not really anything. I love her and everything, but it's never what I want. I don't know. I guess I'm just not ready. For anyone . . . I just don't want to be alone."

He drifted off, and we fell asleep miles apart, separated by an arm's length. His ambivalence was no comfort as I listened to the silence between us.

A few hours later the phone rang, and Jim reached over me to answer. It was Pam, calling from England. I was shocked to hear how angry and curt he sounded.

"Don't you realize it's the middle of the night here? It's after three in the morning! Call back when I'm awake," he ordered, slamming the phone down.

After a spell of plagued sleep, the phone rang again. It was morning now, and Jim was nicer.

"Hello, honey," he crooned, the easy familiarity jolting me with pain.

Fully awake, I grabbed my clothes and climbed out of his bed. I dressed hurriedly in the attached sitting room, listening to their inane conversation: which airline had the best food and whether or not she was old enough to gamble.

After they hung up, it took Jim a while to notice I'd moved to the sitting room. I couldn't stop myself from smoldering.

"Would you like cab fare home?" he asked.

"No," I said. I wasn't being paid for anything.

"Well, would you like a ride anywhere? I can't drive, so the secretary's picking me up. She can drop you off somewhere."

"No, thank you."

"It's not any trouble." Jim kept up his reasonable attitude, but I wasn't interested in being reasonable. "Well, what are you going to do, then?" he persisted.

"I'll think of something!"

He sighed. It was clear—even to me—that I didn't know what I was doing. Jim took a shower, brushed his teeth, and dressed. When he finished, he came back and gave me a long, exasperated look, as if I was beyond belief and he wasn't.

"OK, I'll take a ride to Bel Air," I said. He nodded, appearing to be amiable. It was still hard to resist the urge to trip him as we walked downstairs. Climbing into the car, Jim introduced me to the secretary-driver. "This is Judy. She needs a ride to Bel Air." His tone made me sound like a lunatic. The girl smiled politely and turned up the radio full blast. Jim tapped his fingers on the car roof, in perfect time to the music, as if it was yet another wonderful morning.

"Which girlfriend are you going to visit?" he asked politely, turning to face me.

"He isn't a girlfriend. I'm going to a boyfriend's. His parents are in Europe." This ended all further attempts at communication. I spoke only in directions to the secretary. Once we drove up Stone Canyon, something in me relaxed, enclosed in the long winding tunnel of familiar green trees. "You can pull in here," I said.

I climbed out of the car and pointedly thanked the girl for the ride. Full of confusion, I looked at Jim, unable to decide if I should scream "I hate you" or "I love you." I wished we could be friends for a minute, but he wasn't looking too receptive.

"See you later," I said stiffly.

He gave me a frozen smile, and I walked away.

Strange Days

When Jim dropped me at Bob's doorstep, I heard my name called from the pool amid splashing and laughter. Through the side gate, up the grassy slope, and past the rose garden, happy, tan, and stoned people greeted me as if it were a surprise party. Some were friends from the past, others strangers. I vaguely explained that my car had broken down and Linda needed to pick me up. Everyone thought this was great; Linda would add to the sunny reunion.

Bob ushered me off to the guesthouse for a bathing suit and a phone. Though I'd told Jim that he was a boyfriend, he was mostly just a friend. As we walked, I muttered under my breath. "That was Jim who just dropped me off. He can't even drive his own car."

"That blue Mustang just leaving the driveway was Jim?"

"Yeah. . . . He was awful, just totally rotten. He doesn't have any feelings. Besides that, he's weird."

"Oh, you love it," Bob laughed.

"No, I don't."

"Well, anyone who sings about the Queen of the Angels . . ." Bob shot me a look. "You knew you were playing with fire. Come on, forget about him. Change clothes and call Linda."

Moments later, floating on a raft in the lagoon-type pool, fingers trailing in the blue-green water, I was hit by total incongruity. Dawdling on a beautiful summer day, surrounded by lush foliage, rose gardens, and pretty people, my heart seemed a stone pit. I wasn't the same old crazy Judy who'd do anything. My fingertips traced liquid paths; after a few mirroring undulations, nothing was left, the pattern was gone: nothing lasts.

My attention shifted to Belle, the black lab, retrieving balls from the deep end of the pool. When Linda arrived, she acted cheerful as hell, merrily chiding me for abandoning my car. But once she saw my face, she was careful not to ask any questions. By the time we left Bel Air, we had planned a psychedelic reunion with Bob and Sam. We four were the original take-acid-and-revel-in-the-garden cohorts. Against my better judgment, we agreed to drop it next week at the beach.

Equipped with Orange Sunshine—LSD mixed with STP—Bob and Sam arrived on schedule. With considerable authority, Bob informed us that it'd be "an unforgettable experience," though I wasn't so interested in unforgettable experiences since my arrest. Linda agreed; walls breathing, paisley trails for days were getting passé. This only convinced Bob we had all the more reason for a fresh perspective. We looked at each other and shrugged. What the hell . . .

After swallowing my oversize pill, I walked to the beach alone. The sunset blazed red-orange and magenta, misting over the ocean. The Corona del Mar beach was familiar; I felt at home digging my toes into the cooling sand. As my knotted stomach got tighter, I grew more engrossed with silver veins of water creating canyons in the sand. Waves left salt lines and thrust brown strips of seaweed onto the beach. When I cracked the glistening bulbs open, stored water trickled out, filtering back to the sea. The weed was like a wet animal, its body extended, long arms clutching the sand; if it didn't let go into the tide, it would dry, deaden, and be discarded. Uneasy, I saw it was almost dark and walked back up the hill.

Back in the house, I still had the anxious knot in my stomach. Linda did, too. Bob hadn't mentioned this symptom.

"Just wait a little while," he assured us. "Or you could always take some more."

This was meant as a joke, but Linda and I thought it was the perfect solution.

"Remember," he warned, "this wasn't my idea."

I was gazing out a window at the quiet evening when some moron blasted the room with Jim's scream. The indelicacy. I was working on forgetting him; now his soul ricocheted off the walls, ranting about the "Unknown Soldier." Military killers lined up, one-two-three, robots of death set up the soldier, and . . . wham, he was dead, blood and gore splattering as the militia retreated. Church bells rang, and Jim yelled, "It's all over, all over, all over!"

Linda walked across the room, her eyes berserk. "Let's get out of here!" she said.

We escaped into a bathroom, shutting out the sound. Taking off our clothes, we stepped into the shower, turning it full blast so the hot water soothed us. Showers were safe, sane, and soapy. After a while, we felt better, more stoned, perhaps, but new and clean: there were no wars. When our fingers wrinkled to grotesque proportions, we got out. Wrapping ourselves in fluffy towels, we plopped on the tiled floor.

After a polite knock on the door, Sam whispered, "Are you accepting visitors?" He was a dear old maniac, so we let him listen to our curled-up gossip. He handed me my washed and dried jeans and laughed. I had gotten them sopping wet and sandy while reveling in the seaweed. Assured we were merely blithering idiots in need of a meal, we put our clothes back on.

In the kitchen, Bob and Sam played with spices while they cooked. We were introduced as the Shower Girls to three guys; one had the stereo, the offending record, and the house. They were members of a band called Sons of Champlin that Sam managed in San Francisco. I felt so sick of bands. I stared at Bob in consternation.

"You're a mirror of everything. I just have to look in your face to get a reflection," Bob said.

I walked out of the room to see myself in a real mirror. He was deluded; I had a perfectly distinct face, not some mass conglomeration of others. The four of us trooped into a bedroom and shut the door so the music couldn't invade us. Spared that, we sprawled across the bed to make fun of the world and ourselves, wrapped in delighted mockery when the band members walked in. Another wail of Jim's blasted us, and I clammed up. Everyone else got quiet, too.

"Say something scornful, Judy," Bob urged.

"Hair and cloth, woven images," I mumbled, confused and off guard.

"That's very sensual sounding," Linda said.

But that was it, sensual images, strangers, and Jim. Without warning, I flipped. "Where are my keys?" I asked distrustfully. "Who has my keys?"

No one answered; the silence seemed malevolent. In terror, I believed the earth enforcers were after me again, wanting to punish me for laws I kept breaking. The house had been invaded. I jumped off the bed and ran out to the street. Noises echoed after me and then faded. I found myself on a ledge of earth overlooking the ocean. It was quiet except for my panting.

"Are you all right?" a timid voice asked. Linda was sitting beside me.

"No," I burst out. "I'm scared."

"What is it? Those guys? I mean—you just suddenly ran away!" She put her arms around me because I was crying.

"I've seen too much too fast. I'm going to be punished. I'm going to die for knowing," I confessed.

"You know you aren't literally going to die." Linda looked frightened, but her voice was calmly mystical. "When my roommate got into meditation too fast, this happened to him. He used to be afraid. He was real susceptible to things, too. He just had to slow down for a while. Besides," she continued rationally, "we've got this drug in our systems—that's what's causing everything. We just have to wait for it to wear off."

"Don't leave," I said, slightly comforted.

"I won't. Don't worry," she said. "You know, we could go to a hospital. They'd give us something to come down."

"Oh, no! No, I'll be fine. I don't want to do that again." Sterile white images flashed as I noticed a light on the night horizon, a judging cosmic eye, in league with the earth law enforcers. I'd stay under the control of these forces forever, never to escape the cycle, not even in death, an invention like time. Everything had happened before, all variations on a theme; we'd been everyone; we were everything. I couldn't say this, so I acted composed, suggesting we return to the house, where I might be less vulnerable.

Inside, everything had become symbolic, down to the shadows beneath the lampshades. I walked down a hall covered with green paintings, lush forests that trembled, beckoning for my entrance. Of course, I was too smart for that; I wouldn't get trapped in there for eternity. At the end of the hall, I found a room and walked inside. Surrendering to fate, I lay down on a bed. I hoped my cooperation might win some kind of pardon. It probably got tiring chasing and capturing stray disobedient souls.

When I looked up, I saw the framed face of Jesus on the wall. I'd never identified with him much, but from the expression in his eyes, I could tell he'd come to save me. He forgave people like me, which was consoling; he was also an intermediary between the dark forces after me. Whenever I heard threatening sounds outside the room, I looked at him for reassurance that they wouldn't get me.

Nothing happened. No one came to take my life. I looked out at the vines weaving unperturbed nocturnal life. A loud clock ticked beside the bed; there was time again. The timeless forces had missed their chance to abduct me, lost their power—like a full moon leaving the werewolf a human. My eyes fell on a Cinderella book on the floor, and I heard my own involuntary laugh. She was still waiting for her prince, too. I'd awoken to Cinderella and the clock, my so-called reality.

I walked out, besieged by questions. I said I was fine, just fine. But I felt very, very old. Linda talked with Bob and Sam about what should be done; they decided I should be taken home. I followed directions and got in Linda's car, staring at the half-dark grayness called dawn.

At home, I found I shouldn't be there. It was four in the morning, I was in a borderline psychotic state, and my mother was awake. I illustrated nonverbal thoughts by drawing trails across the air, swirling with magical twists of my arms, hands, and body, Isadora Duncan beyond reason. After watching long enough to determine I was harmless, Mom closed her bedroom door and left me alone to come down.

I danced around a while longer; then I turned to Duffy. He'd been watching, too, from long-lashed terrier eyes, but in a mild, nonjudgmental way. Sitting on the couch together, we put our heads under the drawn curtains and gazed outside. We nuzzled each other in understanding, watching early light filter into the garden. He was the most intelligent creature I'd run across all night. The deep green of the plants was dewy as the flowers opened to morning.

After the sun turned the world to day, my eyes fell on a *Time* magazine. This seemed almost comic—in the corner, I read the words "August 1968." Apparently that was the present, though it sounded like years before. I was eighteen. I lived in California, where nothing lasted and everything remained new. Headlines had proclaimed God was dead when God seemed beyond and between birth and death. Everything and nothing was what I had left to believe in. I walked to my bedroom and collapsed in exhaustion.

It was the last time I ever took LSD.

Sympathy for the Devil

If I didn't know better, I'd think you were Catholic," Dr. Atkins told me in the hospital. "The guilt! I'm just wondering why you felt you should be punished." He was Jewish, so the allusions confused me.

"But I didn't. They did!" I said impatiently. "I'd broken the earth laws, like thought crimes, and they had to get me . . . like when I was arrested, only this time it was a cosmic force after me."

"I just want you to consider that they came out of your mind," he said gently.

"You think I'd want to punish myself? That's really sick!" It especially irritated me that he didn't understand I was innocent.

"You remember the story about the tree of knowledge—original sin? Some people don't buy that one anymore. . . . So, you knew why you would be punished?" He sounded mildly ironic.

"For thinking the wrong things," I said. "For doubting too much and not believing the right way. Knowing too much without being ready for it." But I was already trying to figure out what he'd meant; it seemed so long ago that I'd heard that story.

For Christmas 1966, our last as a family, I'd gone to St. Andrew's church with Mom and Rosalie. We sat in the hard wooden pews, heavy gilt hymnals in hand when we stood to sing. I never liked the singing: all that standing up and sitting down. It was bad enough that I couldn't carry a tune, but Rosalie sang so high and clear that her soprano soared out over everyone's heads. Embarrassed, I gazed down at her soft white hands and billowy chiffon dress as her gently rounded bosom heaved with zeal. In that moment, her navy print dress seemed as hopelessly dated as her seamed silk stockings and head-hugging cloche.

I'd scrunched down when the pastor gave a sermon on Doubting Thomas, uneasily concluding I was just like him, wanting to stick my fingers in Christ's wounds for proof he'd come back. My skepticism felt harrowing as the pastor's dark eyes fixed intently on mine. Cautious agnostics, my parents doubted God existed but wanted me to decide for myself. After that service, at Rosalie's concerned prompting, I pledged to become involved in fellowship every week. My sense of guilt was so well honed that this seemed a last chance to save myself.

My period had started in church on Easter Sunday. I'd felt twinges of pain, spasmodic pangs as I began bleeding halfway through the morning service. Blood seeped as I watched the sunlight saturate the red and blue stained glass. I was not only leaving childhood, but my body—my gender—was expelling me from the garden. It was Eve's old punishment, similar to the way girls who developed early seemed like sluts. The injustice was bodily, impersonal—having nothing to do with one's essence—yet each girl no longer seemed an equal but defective. I, too, had fallen from grace, touched by original sin, permeated with it. The only hope offered was the love of a dying god, a resurrected savior.

One night in eighth grade church fellowship, I'd foolishly let it slip that I hadn't been baptized, and one of the teachers took me aside. We sat down at a Formica table, and she grasped my hand. "You really haven't been baptized, dear?"

"No," I said, immediately sorry for admitting it.

"You should speak to your parents. I'm sure they wouldn't want you going to hell."

"I'll really go to hell?" The old-fashioned concept conjured up a profoundly nightmarish image: a black and burning underground where lost souls, damned and shrieking, were chained in flames as a horned devil, not merely a delinquent angel, reigned with a bloody trident. Much worse than Hades, hell was forever, the same as heaven.

"Yes, honey. That's what it says in the Bible."

"Everyone who isn't baptized goes there?" I repeated in disbelief.

She nodded. "Just talk to your parents about it," she said, squeezing my hand and standing up. "They'll do the right thing." She smiled.

The last church activity I attended was a dance in the room that held weekly fellowship, the same room where I'd been told of my impending doom. I kept leaving the dance floor since the kids weren't dancing the jerk, or even the vaguely outmoded twist, but the cotillion-proper box step. Devouring chocolate cupcakes in the drafty kitchen, my friend and I giggled about how old-fashioned everyone was. Guys were not only supposed to make all the moves, but they were also supposed to know how to flirt, too, so these Christian boys seemed hopelessly backward. Their hair was too short, their skinny bodies too awkward. With no easy joking lines, they seemed grim and puritanical—and they were definitely not good dancers. I felt sorry for their stiff, gawky ways, but I also felt exasperated.

With a stoic sense of defeat for my doubt, I rejected fellowship and traditional religion. Later, I'd imagine if I hadn't made out with so many boys, I might have controlled fate through God and kept my parents happy together. When I became involved in Eastern religions, I'd naively claim to be untouched by guilt, that I didn't "understand" the concepts of original sin and punishment, though they had cut to the core of my shame, fear, and rebellion. But in my diary, I just blew it all off, labeling myself "dense and in the dark ages"—and, for many years, I didn't look back.

My Back Pages

Early in the fall of 1968, I searched L.A. for a place to live while I went to art school. In my fantasy, it would be high in the hills, secluded by pine trees, built of wood and stone, with a cozy fireplace. Jim and I would unite as the unparalleled lovers of our time; he'd come for candlelight dinners as we planned a brilliant future. After graduating in four years, I'd achieve artistic acclaim as he continued his poet-singer thing. Married blissful geniuses, we'd travel at times but mostly just create, famous in non-competitive fields. Of course, already having the money, he could pay the rent, or whatever . . .

When I was younger, our version of playing house was anticipatory: my friends and I cooked. My favorite recipe, the Jolly Breakfast Ring, made of Bisquick, milk, and eggs, topped with crushed pineapple and glazed with brown sugar. The golden ring, carefully turned upside down after it baked, came out crumbly and delicious. We finished with broiled grapefruit, which was also covered with brown sugar and then topped with a maraschino cherry. The cherry in the middle seemed grown-up and elegant, like our parents' favorite drinks.

As we cooked, the song "Johnny Angel" played, the romantic soundtrack to our yearning: "Johnny Angel /

How I want him / How I tingle when he passes by . . ." At the end of our cooking, waiting, and wanting, the promised future was coming nearer—in the form of a beautiful, perfect boy whose angel's eyes and lips and touch would transport us like God or Zeus or Jesus to heaven. It was a quest I still took to heart.

Despite all that, I wasn't exactly the domestic type. I got Ds in homemaking, which may have been kind on my teacher's part. I collapsed soufflés, burned hot chocolate, and sewed lopsided seams on my gym bag. When we had our final Home Ec. test, a staged formal dinner to which we invited a guy as a surrogate husband, I blew it. At the height of the solemn main course, I cracked up laughing, spitting milk across the table. The ideal hostess would not conduct herself this way; I was asked to leave the room. The teacher said my saving grace was being the "dramatic type." Maybe if I soared around in a black cape, some fool of a man would propose before my looks burned out.

Except for an occasional English, drama, or art class, I'd lost interest in school beyond friends and boys. Civics was so boring that I sniffed Energine to stay awake. Teachers called me aside, saying they'd seen my IQ and SAT scores. Why did I get such average grades when I was so intelligent? I didn't know. Maybe if I were paid higher prices for my As, I could go to USC and marry a doctor like the other girls. At a time when girls still prepared for life by making dinner, sewing, and learning household tips, I wouldn't be equipped and already didn't care.

ᗢ

The first day of registration at art school, I met Kathy. Her last name started with "Hub," so she stood before me in line. I lightly kicked her leg to get her attention, and she turned around, large brown eyes shocked. I was surprised myself; she was actually wearing a bra under her blouse and carried an efficient looking purse. She looked like a lost secretary surveying me through long, dark hair and freckles as she answered my questions. After mocking the pop-art walls and psychogirl in front of us, we shared our common plight. It would be financially easier to live with a roommate than alone.

Later, when I admitted she seemed like a frazzled secretary, she said I looked like a hippie-surfer-cowgirl. She had a good excuse: she'd just spent nine months recuperating from flipping out in Europe, and the conservative disguise made her feel normal. Neither of us wanted to live in the MacArthur Park area near school; just driving by was enough. Alcoholic, crazed, or just plain unlucky, the people muttered at street gutters lined with muddy papers; they looked as flat and lifeless as the posters glued upright to the peeling green benches. Like Buddha's first lesson after leaving the palace, the aged, sick, and dying lay discarded and forgotten here. If life was suffering, we didn't want to know it yet.

Kathy and I managed to find a small house in Laurel Canyon that almost matched my fantasy. Everything was fine until I brought in my first carload of boxes, mostly books. Walking up the front steps, I was blocked by the landlord, who was making frenzied gestures. Oblivious to the weight of my balanced boxes, he stood a few feet above me, face beet red as he sputtered.

"Your check bounced. Get away—I won't have liars and cheats in my house! There's no telling what you'll do." His cheeks changed from red to magenta to purple—very disconcerting next to his snow-white hair.

"I don't see how it could have bounced." I backed away, worried he'd have a heart attack. "There has to be a mistake. What good would it do to give you a bad check?"

"How can you stand here and lie like that? You girls are just bad. I'm glad I found out before you moved in. Now get out!"

This seemed so unfair, and I cried as I spoke: "But Kathy's dad wrote it. He's a CPA."

"You aren't getting anywhere using those phony tears! Don't think I haven't seen that before!"

"I am not a phony," I said, going cold. This man must have had a rotten love life; no wonder he couldn't trust a soul. "I would never even bother to write you a bad check, and if you can't understand that, well . . ."

"Leave me alone!" he motioned wildly. "Get away from here!"

I picked up my heavy boxes, threw him my most polished glare, and walked away. He was still screaming at my back as I drove off, his arms waving frantically. Turning the corner, I was overcome by tears. The utter cruelty and injustice of it all! Driving down Laurel Canyon in rush hour traffic, I knew I was about to see Jim.

He was walking alone, down a side street near his recording studio. I was in no mood to reflect on intuition; I simply pulled my car over.

"Jim!" I called from the window.

He looked mildly astonished but recovered with expert skill and got into my car.

"Hi, Judy. How are you?" he said, as if it had been three days, not three months, since we last saw each other.

"Terrible," I sniffed. "This horrible thing just happened to me."

"I'm sorry I acted so cold to you last time," Jim said, oblivious to my remark. "But I thought you were starting to act too possessive."

"If I'd had any sense, I would've just gotten mad and left." Me—acting possessive? He was acting like an iceberg—or worse.

"Do you want to go somewhere for a drink?" Jim asked.

"No, not really." I would have liked a drink but worried I'd get hassled, since I was only eighteen. Also, I was on my way to my grandmother's for dinner. Both these reasons seemed too embarrassing to admit.

Jim just sat there, sodden as hell, clearly wanting a drink.

"Something awful just happened to me," I restated, and launched into my landlord story. "Won't you just hold me?" I asked. Jim made a halfhearted attempt, though it was awkward with all the damn boxes. My story seemed to have cheered him up considerably.

"Has Kathy ever lived away from home?" he asked, not waiting for my answer. "Her father probably doesn't want to lose her and wrote the bad check so he could keep her."

"No," I said. "That's not it." Boiling it all down to a reverse Electra complex seemed ridiculously over-Freudian. It also implied that Kathy and I were babies.

"I don't mean he'd do it consciously. He'd just do it," he said with all-knowing authority. Seeming touched by my plight, he now moved the boxes to kiss me. This was beyond anything resembling paternal concern. I felt rebellious and resistant, but my attraction to him took over. He lodged my hand firmly between his legs and then tried to unzip my pants. This was impossible; we couldn't make it in a small car full of boxes. It wasn't even dark yet. I pulled away before he convinced me we should do it on the sidewalk.

"You know, you've always been good to me, in bed." Jim said. "I want to keep seeing you. But it can't be all the time, you know. I can't go with you or anything. That's just the way I am. . . . I'm not dependable; I can't be a real boyfriend. It would just be a few nights together every few weeks or so. Could you do that? I mean, could you handle it that way? I don't want you to get hurt."

Already hurt, I figured I didn't have much to lose. But I also felt he was challenging my strength, asking if I could handle it.

"That's fine," I said, offhand, and he looked pleased with my casual attitude toward this aspect of his character.

"Well, just think about it a while. Then call me tomorrow and give me your new number," he said. "That's a nice outfit you're wearing," he added. "You really have good taste in clothes." He looked bashful and weird, as if this was some mysterious feminine art.

"Thanks," I said, suppressing the urge to laugh. I'd picked out the straightest outfit I owned—a blue suede vest, crepe blouse, and herringbone pants—to impress the landlord. Now, instead, it was impressing Jim. At this rate, he'd get along with my conservative father, which was no mean feat. "I'd better go now. I'm already late for dinner."

"Yeah, I'm supposed to be back in the studio," Jim said, straightening up from his slouch. I brushed my hair back into place. Reaching over to ruin it again, he kissed me, teasing. "Don't forget to call," he said, getting out of the car.

Since I'd moved to L.A., I ate dinner at Rosalie's once a week. As I walked down the ivy-latticed driveway to her door, I sang "Someday Soon." She still lived in the secluded Hollywood cottage she'd moved into more than twenty years earlier: the same lush rose garden bloomed under her window, the hardy strawberry plants she lovingly tended. That night she was making roast chicken, mashed potatoes, and green beans for dinner. I could smell egg custard baking in the oven for dessert. She seemed happy to see me, and I was glad. The simple comfort of domesticity came easily to Rosalie.

"What was that you were singing?" she asked as I came inside.

"It's kind of a country love song by Judy Collins," I said. "About a cowboy."

"You have a pretty voice. You should sing more often."

Then I told her I'd just seen Jim on Willoughby, her side street. I left out the details, but Rosalie knew about love, the old-fashioned kind. She'd saved all the letters my grandfather wrote when they were courting: thin, yellowed envelopes tied with a blue ribbon. Afterward we watched TV, she in her Sears rocker and me at the tiny maple table. Sometimes, if we were both tired, we'd lie down beside each other on her soft double bed, hold hands, and stare up at the peach ceiling as if watching the sunset.

As the only child of an only child, I had my mother and her mother's beliefs sink into me as if they were my own. Later, I'd be shocked to find most of what I believed was not original, wasn't even mine, but something that had seeped in without a thought. When I started driving to Hollywood to see the bands on Sunset Boulevard, I thought I was breaking away, beginning anew. When I fell in love with a pale, dark-haired singer, it barely crossed my mind that my father had been a handsome, moody, dark-haired singer or that I was reclaiming a life my parents lost when I was born. Even my decision to become a fine artist was a continuation of their old argument.

But as I drove home from my grandmother's that evening, all I pondered was how to handle Jim without heartache. The only solution was to never expect anything, but I couldn't do that, either. I was too uncool. Later that night, I gave myself away by dreaming I'd finally won him over with sex and we had to explain it all to Pam.

The next day I dutifully called him during my lunch break. "Is Jim there?"

"Yes, but he's busy rehearsing downstairs."

"Oh. Is Bill there?"

"This is Bill." He sounded suspicious.

"Bill—it's Judy!" I said, expecting recognition.

"Judy who?" He sounded even more suspicious.

"You know, Judy from Linda and Judy?"

"Oh, Judy. There are so many weird people calling here asking for Jim that I never know. How are you?"

"Pretty good. I'm supposed to give Jim my new phone number. Do you want to take it?"

"Sure. I'm going downstairs now and I'll give it to him."

We talked a little more; I hadn't said much about Jim and me but guessed he already knew. After we said goodbye, I felt frustrated. I'd probably have moved by the time Jim called back. But I wanted him. Anything was worth a try.

Love the One You're With

Dr. Atkins listened quietly, tipping his fingers into a little tent beneath his chin. "How did you feel when Jim said you seemed too possessive?"

"Insulted. I was embarrassed; I'd learned not to be that way. It seemed so outdated and lame . . . so unevolved. I thought I was free." Even in the hospital, I was defensive about this; I had a reputation to defend.

"So you felt OK seeing him the way he wanted. Since there was a sexual revolution, you shouldn't be possessive?"

"Well, yeah. I started seeing this other artist, too, just to even things out a little." That was the strategy I'd adopted in high school, playing one guy off another. It had worked pretty well, until it didn't.

An older boy in my neighborhood had shown me the ropes. Class heartthrob, captain of the football team, a senior, Steve remained my neighborhood boyfriend no matter who my official boyfriend was. Our relationship wasn't actually secret, but it wasn't public like my other boyfriends, either; our encounters were a parallel reality, like a dream I never understood, a virginal prototype of what happened with Jim. When I thought of my relationship with Steve, so based on physical attraction, I barely

129

remembered a word we said. Words were irrelevant. Besides, I kept diaries.

I can remember lying in the bedroom, his weight on me as I stared up at the ceiling. A crack of yellow light crept under the door and music played, sadly muted from the living room. The sinking sensation in my stomach tightened as I said the dread words: "I don't want to be used."

A dependent neediness came over me, caving into the wheedling sense of a lie. A large part of me didn't even feel used; I liked our warm physicality as much as he. My words turned my role into the weaker one, pleading for a show of respect another part of me thought was bullshit. My attempt at propriety seemed to cheapen what we had and my sense of self. However, I'd temporarily forced his hand, and later I wrote down his words: "I promise I won't hurt you again, mentally or physically. I won't let you down. I was just confused before."

A few weeks later, he updated his strategy. "You're too serious!" he said. It would be easier if I could see that being together was for fun, or as he so eloquently put it, "for kicks." Sure, I thought, I want to have fun. . . . My brain slowed down, grew cool and distant, considering. I grudgingly admired his objectivity and detachment, his seeming ease—so close to the way I felt, but not quite. Despite simply liking his skin and my new understanding of "just having fun," I still wanted more; it was at odds with my urge for liberation. Steely inside, I vowed to be more like him. Only I couldn't do it, not really, not like a guy, although I'd try for years—decades, actually.

Piece of My Heart

Kathy and I found another place to live, in West Hollywood—what I thought of as Jim-land. It wasn't really an apartment or a house; we rented the other half of a designer lamp store catering to Beverly Hills ladies. A white-haired woman and her ancient German shepherd lived in the rambling old house next door. Though she was shy and reclusive, she sometimes left fresh nut bread on our doorstep. There was also an endless supply of gorgeous men driving up and down Robertson Boulevard; they made a great background.

"Yeah, and they're all gay," Kathy said.

"Oh, come on. They can't all be gay."

"Yeah, all of them. Or practically all of them."

"How do you know?"

"I can just tell." She shrugged; then she glanced at me as if I was remarkably naive. Kathy was particularly adept at spotting gay men, and our street corner was a major meeting place. The barely disguised hook-ups seemed oddly refreshing; ambling along abstractedly, they gazed into interior decorating shops, looked at the sky, walked their dogs. Then, almost accidentally, there were two men instead of one before a store window. It seemed so civilized compared to most guys I'd known. But by the second night, I was bored enough to use earplugs to block out the courtship sounds.

As we were driving home from art school one afternoon, I asked Kathy to take an alternate route up La Ciénega. I felt irrationally certain Jim would appear any minute, I told Kathy. She made a face and said, "I know."

Two blocks later, we saw him. Wearing a straw Mexican hat and a beard, he crossed the intersection before us. Kathy's mouth fell open, and I jumped from the car. Heedless of the honking traffic, I ran across La Ciénega and emerged on the sidewalk, panting and wild-eyed.

Jim had watched from the safety of the curb. He looked me up and down and smiled serenely.

"Want to go for a walk?" he asked, not missing a beat.

"Where?"

"Around the block. I've got some time. Why don't you give me your address now before I forget?" Flourishing his black notebook and a pen, he wrote down my new numbers.

As early dusk settled in the neighborhood, we walked to the corner and turned down a quiet side street. Winter leaves stirred in the light breeze and crunched beneath our feet. I felt as if we'd been transplanted into a small Midwestern town. Jim's face molded softly into a rare peaceful expression as we circled back to the boulevard. We hesitated, but noise intruded, interrupting the mood. Red and green lights flashed chaotic warning signals from the curb.

Waving avidly, a woman and her blonde daughter approached. They were carrying souvenirs from Elektra, Jim's record company. "Oh, you're Jim!" the mother exclaimed with the triumph of a tour guide. "May we have your autograph? We both just love your songs!" She smiled as her bashful adolescent daughter blushed and stared at the ground.

"Why, thank you. Do you have any favorites?" Jim asked, stroking the darkening stubble on his cheeks.

"'The Crystal Ship,'" the mother said enthusiastically.

"Are you growing a beard?"

"Uh, let's just say that I'm trying it out." Jim shrugged. He wasn't just polite but terribly charming, transforming himself into an official star. "I may shave it off tomorrow," he confessed.

"Oh no, please don't!" she begged, enlisting her speechless daughter for help. Pretty and pained, the girl nodded.

I had to retreat. Doing deep breathing exercises, I slunk off to lean against the building and look bored. I imagined it was a foreign language film with occasional, jarring blasts of English. When they walked away, charmed to tears, I fought back a desire to tell them he was a maniac.

"They seemed nice," I said noncommittally.

"Weren't they?" he said, looking enthralled.

"The girl was really pretty."

"The girl? Oh, no—I liked the mother!" he glanced wistfully over his shoulder.

Aimlessly propelled by his bliss and my disorientation, we walked down a back alley. "Come here, look!" he said, motioning toward a building. He stuck his head through the door. "It looks like it's just been deserted!" He sounded excited. "Wouldn't this be a perfect place to fuck? Now, just all of a sudden?"

"Maybe . . ."

Jim slipped inside, quickly swallowed by darkness. Intrigued by the eerie emptiness and wanting him, I followed. "There's even a bed," he said. "See?" He pointed to an amorphous black heap in the center of the room. I ventured to the edge of the dark shape and touched it.

"This is fiberglass!" I cried, running my fingers over it. "I'm allergic to it. I used to get rashes on my stomach from fiberglass boats. It hurts!"

"Then you can just get on your knees and I'll fuck you from behind!" Jim said, throwing his jacket down. "This is for your knees, OK?"

"Yeah, but be careful," I said. I added some of my clothes and climbed onto the heap with mixed feelings. But Jim was in his element, and I wanted to join him. I was willing to be possessed. For a moment. His jacket cushioned my knees, but my shins took the brunt of his weight.

"There's fiberglass embedded in my legs, and they're all itchy!" I said when I could stand again.

"Good. Now you'll have something to constantly remind you of me."

Jim strode across the room, found a bare shelf in the corner, and wrote something in his notebook. I straightened my clothes, brushed my hair, and waited. He just kept writing. I opened and closed my purse, took out my keys and jangled them. Finally I walked over to where he was standing.

"You get so nervous sometimes that you make me nervous, too," he complained, shifting his weight back and forth like James Dean.

"If you'd just let me talk about it, it'd go away," I said. Staring at each other in silence, we simultaneously moved closer. Jim inclined his head sideways to kiss me; then, a fraction of an inch before my lips, he stopped. "We'll both be in Hollywood for a long time. We have plenty of time," he said. Perhaps this was a reason for stopping a kiss that felt like a culmination; he sounded reassured.

"That's true," I said and stepped back. We walked outside; it was sunny, a windy and gorgeous day. The sky was azure, full of amazing white clouds. Feeling light and expansive, I turned to Jim, my arms making a sweeping gesture upward. "It's so beautiful!" I exclaimed, bursting with inexplicable energy.

Jim looked up at the sky, then at the building, and then at me. "This'll be our place," he said.

I wondered about that, but an idiotic happiness filled me anyway; a contagious smile spread across my face. Jim looked puzzled, and his helpless, awestruck expression came teeming over to me—like a shy kid with a crush on a girl. I loved his face, the way it gave him away, unabashed and pure.

Aware of a fleeting power, I threw him a careless, happy smile, and said, "See you." Letting myself be blown freely, I turned down the alley away from him. I floated home in a rhapsody; it took all my concentration not to drift into traffic. When I reached the house, Kathy wanted to go shopping. In a daze, I agreed, and we left to buy print bedspreads, curtains, candles, and flowers.

☙

The next day in painting class, I was handed a note. "Call your mother. Urgent," it said. I asked Kathy to come to the phone booth with me. Mom had just moved to a large house in Laguna with her friend, Bev, who answered the phone and said my mother couldn't talk.

"I don't know how to tell you this, but Duffy is dead," she blurted out. My sweet dog, my loving-eyed friend. Words flowed from the black plastic receiver in my hand, but I couldn't understand them. "It was over in a minute. He was just hit on the side of his head. A little gash, it hardly showed—his body wasn't hurt. He died instantly." I threw away the black object causing my pain . . . Kathy caught it in midair for a factual, unemotional conversation with my mom. Telephone death etiquette: I could talk to my mother's friend, my friend could talk to my mother, but it hurt too much for my mom and I to talk to each other.

I was crying too noisily for the art-school halls, so I ran and hid in the car. Waves of disbelief and tears welled up, rising and falling. No, I thought, not that little brown dog. Not that shy and free creature, so caring, so understanding, so damn trusting. He hasn't been killed by some cold machine, not him . . .

Eventually, a vast silence overtook me. Alone in a parked car in downtown Los Angeles, I gazed at the empty street. Shreds of students' old drawings littered the ground; visions once transformed into art crumbled in the gutter. I felt the emptiness widen, crushing us, each of us glorious and irreplaceable as the tiny purple flowers beckoning from the cracked sidewalk.

Get It While You Can

The next night, I woke from a disturbed sleep, thinking someone was winding a gigantic clock under my window. Time ticked loudly, a hard clicking sound. Frightened, I opened my eyes, but the sound quickly faded. The clock by my bed said 2:15 AM. Hearing a knock on the door, I leapt out of bed. I was alone for the night—Kathy was with her boyfriend. After arming myself with a kitchen knife, I tiptoed to the peephole. It was Jim.

I swung the door half-open, and he smiled sheepishly. "Can I stay with you?" he asked in an orphan's voice. I glanced past him to the black limousine, engine purring as it waited. I focused back on his expectant face.

"OK," I said.

Appearing only mildly drunk, he loped toward the car, motioning for it to leave. I walked back to my bed and waited for him. Stumbling inside, he mumbled "no lights," and fell across me. "Weren't you even going to invite me in?" he asked after a few moments.

"I don't know. I was having a nightmare about this surreal clock."

"You didn't exactly act glad to see me! It doesn't sound like you missed me, either," he said, resting his head in my lap. I was in no utopia myself and shifted impatiently.

"My dog was run over and killed yesterday afternoon," I announced. "Also, my legs have a rash from that fiberglass!" Actually, I had a theory that if I hadn't been with him at four thirty the afternoon before, my dog wouldn't have been run over at the same time. Jim came out of his collapsed position and regarded me with renewed interest. Suffering seemed to perk him up.

"I bet you never expected life could be this hard," he said, stroking my head affectionately. "You're still so young," he added, yearning but heartbroken.

To my surprise, I broke into sobs, and Jim protectively held me.

"Come on, let's pull the sheets back and get in bed," he suggested. "There's nothing else you can do."

Lulled by his tender authority, believing in his voice, hoping he'd make everything right, I obeyed. It seemed poignant; intimate strangers wrapped around each other in a twin bed. The gentle side of Jim felt strong, though I sensed he was about to break into tears. I wanted comfort, not sex, but he wanted to leave the past behind.

"Come on, Judy, let it go. Come on," Jim's hoarse voice pled brokenly. "Let's fuck death away. Now . . . fuck death away!" But I was earthbound, unable to brush off my troubles. His despair seemed to echo off the walls, building out of control until he surrendered with one last anguished call, trading chaos for peace. Relieved, I sank back against the pillows.

We talked softly, sadly, about nothing, really. He seemed curious about my impressions of life, as if my fresh exposure would give him new clues about existence.

He had simple questions I couldn't answer, though I tried. "What's it like for you now, living in the city?"

"It seems sort of bitter," I answered. "No, not bitter, bittersweet." Life wasn't easy, he agreed. But holding me, Jim provided the secure, soothing feeling I needed, and we floated off to sleep.

∽

When we woke, daylight felt brash and glaring, too sudden. Jim was nice to sleep with, close and warm, but he had drifted away. Immobile, he stared at the ceiling, hard and incommunicative. Worried, I looked up at the ceiling, too. Some fool had sprayed it with silver glitter flakes, possibly under the illusion that tinsel resembled sparkly stars.

"That ceiling's horrible," I said, my words piercing the silence.

He didn't respond; his eyes were stony, walls of blank refusal. I was afraid to ask what was wrong. Under Jim's grim scrutiny, everything seemed so grotesque that I got out of bed. Oddly, that jolted him back to life. He smiled amiably.

"Can I use your shower?" he asked, looking dazed.

As Jim showered, I dressed quickly, made the bed, and prepared to face the reality of my dead dog in Laguna. He came out of the bathroom looking fresh and cheerful. "It's so clean and pleasant here," he said. "Could I have something to drink?

I made him a big mug of chocolate Nestle Quik. "This is the best thing I've had in ages!" he said, greedily drinking it down. I couldn't believe how simple he could be. But as quickly as this passed, he swooped back toward depression. "I guess I'll have to call a taxi. Can I use the phone?" he asked forlornly.

"I can drop you off somewhere if you want. I've got to go anyway."

"Really? It's only Westwood. It's right on the way to the freeway, too." Jim smiled gratefully. Making a phone call in his business voice, he told someone he'd be there soon and said, "It'll all be worked out."

"It's the first time I've left this apartment for a weekend, so I'm afraid it'll blow up if I forget something," I confessed, scanning the front room. "Have I forgotten anything?

"Make sure the water's off and the heat's off and the gas's off," he sagely advised, and we left.

As we drove through Beverly Hills, Jim threw his head out the window and waved to a small blonde child.

"Hello, little girl!" he yelled exuberantly. She stared back, refusing to acknowledge his greeting. "Snotty kid," he muttered, as if everyone should be happy on such a damp, blue-skied morning. I pulled my floppy felt Greta Garbo hat off and on, trying the slant at different angles.

"I wonder where we'll be ten years from now?" he asked.

"I don't really want to know," I said, throwing my hat in the backseat.

"Oh, you'll probably be married and painting on the side." He spoke as if I had an easy, reassuring fate.

"Oh, right," I said, mimicking the voice of another quaint chick artist on her way to placid domesticity. "When I'm not feeding or diapering my babies, I cook and paint flowerpots on the side." I glared, and he cast me a concerned glance. "You'll probably be married, too."

"Yeah, I probably will be." Jim sighed in resignation. He didn't react properly to hostility. But since he'd more or less admitted he'd succumb to marriage, I temporarily forgave what I thought was deprecation of my art. I wondered whom he thought he'd marry.

"Can I turn on the radio for a minute?" he asked, flicking from station to station. "I have this addiction to seeing whether or not they play our music. They're always fucking you over, so I'm always checking."

He couldn't find his current single—not that he gave it much of a chance—and clicked off the radio. "I'll have to give you a copy of my book. It's really good, and I'll sign it for you. Then, someday when I'm dead, you'll have money since it'll be a collector's item."

I rolled my eyes at him.

"I'm serious, it will be!"

"I believe you," I said, in a deadly serious tone.

"I think what you need is a boyfriend."

I nearly crashed at this insult, but I reined myself in. "Well, I liked this one guy. But he was too stupid for me," I said, thinking of an artist who ruined his image when he forgot what hieroglyphics were.

"Oh, you were just too smart for his games, huh?" Jim chortled merrily.

I remained silent.

"You can't look for it; then it'll never happen. I think it's always an accident, you know. People just meet, and they fall in love, all by accident!"

I tried to figure out what that made us—friends that fucked? My heart sank. I was relieved we'd reached his destination. "Can I come with you the next time you go to Laguna?" he asked. "I really like it down there. It would be like a weekend vacation! I could meet your mother, too."

"Yeah, sure, there's plenty of room," I said, totally confused but slightly hopeful again.

"Have a good weekend," he said, smiling and getting out of the car.

Just as I was pulling away from the curb, Jim loped to my open window and planted a kiss on my lips. Amazing. I drove away, promising myself I'd never try to understand what he said or did again. When I turned on the radio, his new single was playing.

All Along the Watchtower

I felt relieved to return to Hollywood Sunday night. Impermanence, that's all there was. Duffy was gone. Whether things were good or bad, Mom's motto was, "This, too, shall pass." That was true, but sometimes it seemed like an excuse for things to be chaotic all the time. The weekend had been a series of anxious philosophical statements about loss. Life is fleeting; grief is temporary. Just grab a beer and a hot dog and look at the lovely, gleaming sea.

Glad to be alone, I washed and set my hair, a good solid chore that served as a sedative. When Kathy returned, we tried to make sense of her boyfriend's and Jim's behavior. Giving up on understanding either, we went to bed.

Five thirty in the morning brought door slamming, shuffling, and raucous laughter to the front porch. Then there was a knock—more like the sound of a falling body than a hand, but nevertheless, a knock. I opened the door to find Jim collapsed against the wall. When he heard me, he snapped his head to attention and tried to stand without the wall. He was unmistakably drunk.

"We just got back from Mexico," he explained disjointedly, waving at the limo parked sloppily across the street.

Pulling pink curlers from my hair, I frantically threw them behind me. Once I had finished saving my appearance, I listened. Jim was saying he wouldn't have made it back alive without his new savior, the chauffeur, whom he insisted must come in, too.

"But my roommate's here."

Snorting impatiently, Jim bolted from the porch. He staggered across the small front lawn, twirling a Mexican straw hat on one finger. Throwing the hat in the air and catching it with whoops of pleasure, he danced in a lopsided circle. He yelped, lost his balance, and tossed the hat. It landed forlornly on the sidewalk. Performance thus ended, he turned back to me.

"My friend doesn't have anyone; I can't just leave him! Don't you love me?" Jim asked.

"OK. Let me ask Kathy." As Jim walked inside, she sleepily stumbled forward.

"I just had a dream someone was trying to murder me," Kathy said. As she took in Jim, her face filled with embarrassed disbelief.

"That just about cuts the mustard!" Jim retorted, turning melodramatically to leave.

"Oh, come on," I said, catching his arm. "This is my friend, Kathy."

"Hi," she said, rubbing her eyes.

"Kathy," Jim said, seizing her hand. "I have this problem. See, Judy here doesn't want my friend, who drove me all the way home from Mexico, to come inside. Do you think that's fair?" He glanced reproachfully at me.

"What time is it?" she asked.

"Nearly six AM. Time for America to rise and shine!"

"We might as well get up—we're already awake," she noted philosophically. "*Captain Kangaroo*'s on pretty soon."

"Oh, good—let's have a party!" Jim beamed, beckoning to someone from the doorway. Calling to his friend, he jumped off the porch.

"Judy, he's really drunk!" Kathy said.

"Oh, God, I'm sorry." I sighed, leaning against the door. "I've never seen him this bad. Really." My voice dropped as Jim staggered back up the steps, a tall, thin man trailing behind him.

"No lights. No lights!" Jim cried, shielding his friend from the imaginary glare of cameras. "This, ladies," he bowed, gesturing to the man beside him, "is Mayor Sam Yorty's only son, traveling incognito. It's a government secret, of course, so he's impersonating that Latin ladies' man, Don Juan."

Don Juan, mustering a wary smile, collapsed wearily into the corner chair. A long, self-conscious silence followed. Jim weaved back and forth across the room, apparently balancing on an invisible tightrope. Pausing deliberately, he took a graceful spin, nearly tripped, and then retrieved his balance in midair. I was amazed by the grace he maintained, turning stumbles into intentional dance steps while barely conscious.

"This isn't much of a party," he mumbled, glaring pointedly at me. Kathy and I exchanged glances, hardly the early-morning hostesses he had expected. Singing sullenly to himself, he veered into the kitchen. The radio blared full blast; after acknowledging it was a good station, Jim immediately shut it off. The cabinets and refrigerator slammed open and shut. "Nothing to drink," he yelled. Rushing from the kitchen, he cried, "Where's my hat?"

Don Juan, having trouble keeping his eyes open, started to attention. "I don't know, man," he said apologetically.

"Jesus. If there was a woman here, she'd take care of me," Jim said. "She'd give me a bath!"

"Your hat's still on the sidewalk," I muttered.

Jim ran outside, leaving the door open. Stumbling back inside, he flourished his hat and arranged it on Don Juan's head. "A pirate, a cowboy . . . a desperado!" he said, adjusting the brim to fit different characters. "A conquistador," he finally exclaimed, sounding pleased. Don Juan coughed, falling into a fit of wheezing laughter. Then he fell silent as Jim told jokes that lacked punch lines. Responding to one about a blind man with chilling laughter, he finally noticed his unreceptive audience.

"Do either of you have any silk dresses?" he asked. "You know, the kind that drape and cling?"

"Not here," Kathy said. Embarrassed, I looked at the floor.

Jim plunged into a rambling, semipoetic dissertation about the eternal mystery of a woman's body veiled in silk. Kathy shot him dirty looks as I assumed the blank face of a model. He kept talking until she switched on the TV, angrily changing channels until she settled on some cartoons.

"Hey—you can't do that! This is Saint Patrick's Day," he protested, turning off the television. "We're supposed to be celebrating for the wee people of Ireland! Doesn't anyone care?"

"You're a descendant of the leprechauns?" Kathy said, snickering.

"It's not funny—it's the truth! I know it," Jim declared. "In any case, we're celebrating for them." He grabbed his

Mexican reds, split them into meticulous halves. Under the cloak of polite ceremony, we were supposed to swallow these for his ancestry. His harsh insistence left little room for argument. The pills were quickly consumed, bringing no alleviation. Going cold and analytical, I stared at him.

"What are you looking at?" Jim asked.

"Nothing," I said. The contempt in his eyes changed my mind. "Why does everything have to be so bad?" I asked.

"We all have our run-over dogs," he muttered, regarding me scornfully. He turned to Kathy. "We're all lost, aren't we?" he demanded, reaching for her wrist.

"I don't know what you mean," she said, shrugging him away.

"You know what I mean—lost."

"No, I don't." Kathy glared at him and walked into the kitchen.

"Cunt," Jim said, presumably to Don Juan. "I want some of that holy wine with the nun in the field." Laughing caustically, he glanced at me in bewilderment, his eyes holding a mute appeal for mercy.

The run-over dog remark had betrayed my love in one swoop; I lurched up and left the room without a word. In the back bedroom, I climbed into the walk-in closet, closed the door behind me, and curled into a fetal position. I would stay there forever, or until Jim left, whichever came first.

When Kathy found me in the closet, I was clutching a leather emblem of a fire-spitting serpent that I had once embroidered in a reverie over Jim. This wasn't the mythical world I had planned.

"What're you doing in here?" she asked.

"Sleeping on reds."

"We all thought you'd just disappeared!" Her brown eyes were warm with concern.

"Is he gone yet?" I asked, shifting my crouched position on the floor.

"No. He's just given up. We went to the Hollywood Ranch Market. It was the only place open with the right wine, J&B, cheese, and vodka." Kathy sounded suspiciously high.

"Who went?"

"Me and John—that's Don Juan's name. He said Jim doesn't think anyone loves him for his true self. He can't trust anyone anymore. He doesn't think he has any friends!"

"I wonder why," I snorted.

Kathy looked at me reprovingly. "I don't think you're being fair," she said in the measured, liberal tones of an adult. "You could at least be civil and come out of the closet!"

"Is he still drunk and obnoxious?" I asked.

"No, he's real quiet and sad. I told you—he gave up. He thought you'd left. Now he's just sitting there. . . . And I'm getting breakfast together. Besides, I think he likes you," she added, bounding from the room. That was enough to get me off the floor.

Following cautiously, I crept down the hall. *Captain Kangaroo*, Kathy's favorite morning escape, blasted a cheerful drone, easing the tension. TV had its merits. Jim looked at me as if I was a hallucination and smiled.

"Hi, honey, will you make me a cup of coffee?" he purred, as if we were an old married couple, a just-married couple, or at least some kind of couple.

Kathy had gone to the café across the street to buy something deliciously expensive for breakfast. She wanted to make sure poor Jim wouldn't think we wanted him for his money, fame, or sex appeal. The coffee, hash browns, sausage, scrambled eggs, and muffins made him more amiable.

"You're a real champ," he congratulated her.

"Yeah, that's what they called me in high school," she said, putting an unopened fifth of Scotch, vodka, and Blue Nun away, though they were the purpose of the trip to the market.

"I really appreciate what you're doing for me," Jim said, eating ravenously. "I'm so comfortable—I couldn't ask for more!" Growing more docile and sweet by the second, he finished his meal, kissed me on the cheek, and sprawled across the couch. In seconds he was asleep. Emerging from the kitchen where he'd been trying to kiss Kathy, Don Juan followed Jim's cue and conked out on the sofa bed. Oh, the excitement! Appraising the situation, Kathy and I silently looked at each other, tiptoed around the apartment, and fled out the front door.

After discovering reds definitely weren't the thing for painting—my liberated hand ruined any internal logic on the canvas— Kathy and I left our studio class early. The only possible retreat seemed El Carmen, a nearby Mexican café. We ate, woke, and slowly recuperated from the morning. As the hours passed, we dawdled. I felt sorry and heartless. I wanted to love Jim, but I wanted him to go away. Dealing with him threatened my sanity; not dealing with him threatened my existence. The difference was negligible. When we returned home, I hoped Jim was there as much as I hoped he wasn't.

Roadhouse Blues

You mean you just left us here, all alone?" Jim asked when Kathy and I returned home. He and Don Juan were sitting there, looking hung over and woebegone.

"What were we supposed to do? Sit around and watch you sleep?" I asked.

Unable to find a comeback, Jim looked crucified. Feeling like a deserting traitor, I sat beside him in lieu of offering an apology. This trifling gesture apparently caused Don Juan to believe we were finally pairing off. He followed Kathy around, kissing her behind the ears, murmuring Latin lover lies. She called an old boyfriend who invited her to Palm Springs. Don Juan pouted as she packed. When she called her father and made up a story about what she was doing, Jim bolted to attention.

"And I thought I wanted a daughter!" he said in disgust.

Kathy sent Jim her most polished look of scorn. Poor Jim was wearing thin on her. By the time she was leaving, he'd collapsed again, and her attempt to introduce her boyfriend fell on deaf ears. He seemed to regard Jim as a scientific specimen, though his detachment was stripped when Jim loudly said, "Good-bye, good-bye!" Falling upside-down and backward, he waved merrily and chortled. The door closed to Kathy's stifled giggling.

I wanted to wake Jim up, so I kissed his face. Infantile, he responded with gurgling childlike noises. Alarmed, I stared at him with sacrilegious revulsion. Suddenly I didn't like the mole by his nose, or his ears, and I wondered what I'd ever seen in him. With a mournful sigh, Don Juan lurched from the corner, cast me a greedy look, and nodded good-bye so as not to wake the baby. As the engine turned over outside, Jim awakened, transforming from an inert rock into a lightning rod, and bolted out the front door.

"Stop! Stop!" he yelled, running down the street.

From the front steps, I watched Jim waving his arms—as if to stop the world, not merely his departing friend. Dropping his hands, he sank to the curb with an air of complete dejection. Under the flickering street lamp, he appeared the archetypal lost soul, cold and defeated in the gutter. He looked so wretched and pathetic; I walked out into the damp evening and sat beside him in silence. I didn't know what to say, but he couldn't even speak. We stared at the thin, muddy stream of water trailing down the storm drain.

"Jim, I really do like you," I finally managed.

"Good. I like you, too. Let's go out to dinner," he said. No longer morbid but smiling and slightly giddy, he bounded up from the street. "I know where we can have great Italian food. You'll love it!" he said, humming as we walked across the lawn.

"We're in the city now, we can't go barefoot now," he sang as we walked inside. I laughed, gathering this light-hearted jingle was either a new cowboy song or a subtle hint not to look like I just fell off the turnip truck. As I put on my suede jacket and boots, Jim pulled me over to the mirror and surveyed our appearance as a couple. He smiled hopefully. Then he looked worried. "Are you taller than me?" he asked.

I assured him I wasn't, for at least the fifth time to date. His preoccupation with my height seemed boundless, like I was an Amazon and he was a midget. After we stood back to back so he could check more carefully, he calmed down, and we left the house.

I drove Kathy's car, a big convertible that gave Jim lots of room to sprawl out. He was conducting a long, serious monologue about women.

"They're the noble creatures who carry on your name with dignity after you die. Women are like depths of compassion," he said, nearly swooning with poetic delight. It sounded pretty romantic, for an idea. I'd never felt like a depth of compassion, but maybe I was too young.

"Chicks," he told me, "have a comic approach to life." He sounded puzzled and envious. I could've used a comic approach—especially since I felt misplaced as a female entirely, neither a chick nor a woman. Ladies lived in English castles, so that was out.

"You know," Jim continued, "what I need is a woman who would just laugh at me. One who wouldn't take me seriously. . . . I mean, the things I do—the stupid things— she would just laugh."

This seemed unlikely if you took into consideration the "stupid things" he did. He'd recently been arrested for public indecency, which seemed barely the tip of the iceberg. I glanced sideways to see if he was joking, but he wasn't. He wore the yearning look that accompanied his deepest delusions. Afraid to speak, I listened to gravel crunch under the tires as we pulled into the parking lot.

"You're such a good driver. You know, they still say I'm dangerous." He sighed loudly. "I had to stop. I'm too irresponsible. I just can't concentrate on anything specific that long."

When we got out of the car, the air smelled fresh and clean. Revitalized, we smiled, and everything seemed new again. An older gay guy walked down the narrow gravel alley in front of us. "I wonder how it feels to be an aging homosexual," Jim mused.

"Aging, I guess," I said. "I thought you were bi or something, anyway. Someone said so." I was open and friendly about it; just curious, but he got cold as hell.

"That guy must've been projecting," he said frostily.

"What guy?" I asked.

"The guy who told you that!"

We'd emerged on a busy sidewalk under the bright lights of Dan Tana's, an Italian restaurant. The Troubadour was a few doors down. Jim had stopped walking.

"I'm hopelessly heterosexual," he said dramatically. Judging from his face, this was a terrible predicament. I looked appropriately sympathetic and let the subject drop.

Regaining his composure, Jim led me inside, and we were seated in a corner booth. He soared into a gracious man-of-the-world role, handling waiters and wine with wit and style. We had a drink, and everything seemed romantic, until he discovered all I wanted to eat was soup. "You're not hungry? If you hadn't deserted us and left me alone like that, this wouldn't be happening. I bet all you did was eat all day. It's true, isn't it?"

"No! I'm just not that hungry," I lied. But he was right; I'd stuffed myself at lunch.

"I'll bet it wasn't as good as what you could have here!" he continued.

I ordered the veal piccata. Recuperating with a few sips of wine, he got softer and said maybe he was falling in love with me. "Could you be faithful to me?"

"If I wanted to," I said, secretly thrilled he'd ask.

"No, I'm serious. Sometimes I might leave you a few months at a time. And I want to meet all women. Even her!" He pointed to a loudly dressed, overweight, almost ugly woman across the room. I wrinkled my nose, unimpressed. "But that's it—that's what I mean," he said. "I want to know what she's like. Not her, really, but all women. . . . I can't help it. And I'll bet you could never wait—you could never wait that long."

"I could, too," I blundered, and he won another game.

"Your roommate's really cute. Maybe all three of us could get together sometime."

"No," I answered carefully. This was going further than I wanted. "Kathy wouldn't want to. She tried that once and didn't like it at all."

"She must have liked it," Jim said, using his remarkable logic. "Otherwise she wouldn't remember."

"Why don't you just get someone for me?" I asked, defiantly upping the ante. "I think I'd like that better."

"That wouldn't be quite the same," he mumbled.

"Why not?"

"It just wouldn't be." He shrugged and looked away. "What I want to do is start a new religion. That's what I really want to do. But first," he added, "I want to be a movie star." He made it sound all misty and dreamlike. I'd suspected something like that but was afraid to ask about the basis of his religion.

"Won't that look sort of stupid? I mean, people will laugh—a movie star starting a new religion, you know?" It was already bad enough getting arrested for obscenity.

"Yeah, I know . . ." Jim sounded resigned. "But you know that Frank Sinatra song? The one about getting older and wiser but having done it his way? Have you listened to the lyrics, I mean, really?"

I nodded. Because my father had sung with him, I'd listened fairly intently to Sinatra.

"Well, that's all I want," he said.

If only he weren't so sincere, I thought. If only he didn't care so much. Unhinged by the depth of his dreams, I blurted out my LSD arrest story, emphasizing how I'd felt the blue veins on my wrist were him, were life itself.

"I think you must have gotten that from Pam," he said, before I'd finished. "She has this thing about her hands. She thinks they're going to be cut off or some-thing. A fear of damaged fingers."

"But I don't even know Pam!"

"It would come from me, really—but through her. I'm sure you got it from her." He made it sound simple and obvious, like some psychic venereal disease.

"What's she like?" I didn't really want to know, but I had to ask.

"She's always giving me trouble," he complained. "She's always disturbing me—on purpose. To make me react. She's always trying to make me react."

"Well, that's only . . ."

"So I don't react!" He looked proud of this, but then his irritation turned to guilt. "I mean, she's been everything to me. She's been my mother, my sister, and my daughter, my friend and lover. Every time we start to live together, I'm optimistic. . . . Maybe I'm too idealistic, but it just never works out." He sighed. "I love her. I'm just not in love with her."

I didn't ask for all the gory details and felt nauseated, torn between jealousy and sympathy for Pam. At the same time, I was hopeful. Confused, I retreated.

"I don't feel I've ever seen the real you," I heard Jim say. His voice held a note of challenge.

"That's probably true." I wanted him to see the real me, whatever that was. "I'm really shy," I said, thinking this was a clue.

"You—shy?" Snorting at this impossibility, he traced my breast lightly, as if it proved my daring.

"Yes, I really am," I insisted, drawing back. "Another thing is that I ran away with my first boyfriend. My father hated him because I loved him."

Jim claimed my dad was behaving logically. (I did lose my virginity, didn't I?) Then he crossed over an invisible line, telling me what great sex we were going to have. "What you should do—is just be really luxurious."

"What do you mean, luxurious?"

"Like a little girl, crawling around with that unselfconscious sexuality." I took a moment to digest his definition of "luxury." "Also, I think it would help to just lie around and suck my cock for hours."

"Well, yeah, if I can ever come, too."

"Well, it's hardly like a guy ejaculating!" he said. I glared back, wondering if he knew I'd passed my thirteenth birthday.

"Why did you have to do that 'I Have a Cock' performance in Miami?" I spit out.

"That isn't important! I'm tired of it." Looking defensive, he waved the subject away. I kept staring at him, expecting an answer. He fidgeted under my gaze. Reaching for my hand under the table, he lowered his voice. "I don't know. I just couldn't help it," he said, plaintively searching my eyes, making them soften. I was supposed to be the forgiving, understanding one, jumping out of my identity into his. And I did. The romantic mood was recaptured, though the waiters cast closing-time looks. "They're too blatant! I like to be the last to go," Jim said. Nevertheless, he rose and we left.

We walked next door to the Troubadour. As we went inside, people watched him, and I felt exposed. I hoped they didn't think I was another naive girl who didn't know about him. I wanted to scream, "I know, I know!" When Jim peeked around the corner to see who was on stage, a frenzied cocktail waitress ran up to him.

"Don't start that shit again!" she shrieked. They were obviously old, intimate enemies, and I felt alarmed by her, relieved to escape into the bar. Jim ordered a margarita but announced I was too drunk to have any more. Infuriated, I flirted with a nearby friend of his.

"Is he giving you a hard time?" the guy asked me.

"Cool it," Jim said to him. Icily reducing me to property, he steered me toward a group of overly hip looking men. I quickly surmised they were old drinking partners and felt uncomfortably aware of being female in a totally male atmosphere. Jim's Miami bust had now become "a humorous bit of politics that got out of hand," which he found wildly entertaining.

"I wonder what it'll be like when we're in our thirties and people respect us?" he asked. As Jim looked around the room reflectively, the gray strands in his beard stood out. No one answered. Then he ordered another drink, started the cycle up again, beginning to laugh at nothing.

Taking me aside, he said, "I'm going to be here for a while, and this will just bore you . . . so you might as well go home now, and I'll be back later." He paused uncertainly and looked into my eyes. "I still love you and everything," he vowed. I was shocked. He'd never really said he loved me, and now he loved me still? I smiled weakly, too tired to keep up. Jim was caught up on a new wheel of faces, experiences, and places. He needed an extra dose—an extra dose of everything. I wanted to go home and sleep. If I was just patient, he would come back; he'd realize I was the one for him. He'd show up when the circle was through—this one or the next.

Helpless

I woke up alone the next morning, dressed, and drove to art school. I'd already internalized that artists were tragic characters, and I took it to heart. Teachers praised my "personal, dedicated" paintings and gave me As, but I was mostly dedicated to the creation and upkeep of my fantasy world. That day I'd have done better in a padded cell than the painting studio. When I got home, the phone was ringing, causing me a near breakdown. I jammed my key into the locked door, bolted across the room, and breathlessly picked up the receiver, as if expecting God.

It was a girl's hesitant voice. "Is this Judy?"

"Yes."

"This is the secretary for the Doors. Jim said he may have left his notebook at your house." She sounded apologetic and embarrassed. "Do you know if it's there?"

"Yeah, it's here on the floor somewhere." I had skimmed through it last night and found it nearly incomprehensible. There was poetry, a scrawl proclaiming, "Therefore, time does not exist," and something resembling a screenplay about billboards and bathrooms on Sunset Boulevard.

"They're having a session now. He needs it—there are some new songs in it. Could you possibly drop it off?"

"Sure," I said. I was willing to drop myself off parcel post. "I'm only a few minutes away."

"Oh, thank you. I really appreciate it." She sounded relieved, like I had spared her some horrendous task, and we hung up.

I didn't stop to sit down, breathe slowly, or recollect who I was or what I was doing. I simply plunged ahead without thinking, the habit of impulsiveness driving me. I scanned my appearance and emerged into the world with no sense of gravity. I left his Mexican hat on my floor. A few minutes later, I arrived and handed over his black notebook to the new secretary.

Bill waved me into his office and shut the door. After the polite assurance that I was looking good, he got to the point. "You know, Jim just disappeared for three days."

"I know. He was with me," I answered defensively. Bill shook his head.

"Well, when he left, he was with another girl. I saw her. She was just as good looking as you, and smart, too." He gave me an awful, piercing look. I stared at him, thinking, I'm different.

"But I love him," I said.

Bill opened his door and nodded to the secretary sitting in front. "She loves him, too. She came here all the way from the East Coast."

I inspected her. Then I defiantly stuck out my tongue.

"But he's never given her a reason to believe, like you," Bill said. At least he knew I'd been handed a few measly reasons. Closing the door, he sat down and shook his head again.

"You don't know how many secretaries have had to leave because of him. At first, they think they can save him. Then they see him coming in, raking himself over the coals day after day. No one can really help him. I don't know, either he'll end up a refined, mellow guy or in the gutter. Don't think I don't love him—I've just seen a lot of it."

"But I love him!" I repeated, knowing it sounded ridiculous. I was shaking, and my tears brimmed over.

"I know." Bill's voice sounded hollow. "But I just don't think Jim can really relate to women. Except Pam, I guess. I don't really know what their gig is." He shrugged in distaste. "I don't understand what he sees in her. She's always crying. But she helped him a lot in the old days when he was getting started. It's too bad you didn't meet him back then."

In tears, my pride slipped off in liquid layers; soon it would be a puddle on the floor. Bill got up and wrapped his arms around me. "I just can't give up," I whispered.

Bill didn't answer. I wiped my face and backed off, trying to smile.

"I better leave," I said, getting nervous. I didn't want Jim to see me in this state.

"Take care of yourself." Bill hugged me good-bye, having done his best to warn me.

I walked through the office and down the staircase like a model down a runway. I may have been petrified, sick, held together by loose pins, but no one would ever guess. Unless he happened to meet me halfway through the show, on the landing by the geraniums, like Jim did.

"Hello," he said, in that husky voice.

I couldn't speak. My lungs burst for air; standing seemed a feat in itself. His pleased expression became confused. As the silence mounted, he looked puzzled and expectant.

"Thanks for bringing my book," he said finally. "I would've called or come over myself, but we were really busy."

"You didn't come back," I heard myself say. Only my voice was a hoarse frog's croak that broke at a high, static pitch—embarrassing as the sentence I'd just stuttered out.

"I stayed with some friends."

"Oh . . . I hope you had a nice time." This statement was supposed to seem sincere and cancel out my opening croak; it was supposed to show I had no desire to hamper his freedom. Only it sounded totally phony. I felt like a scroungy dog, caught off guard with a mangy, secret bone. And the secret was terrifying. I'd put everything crucial, ideal, and beautiful into one image. The image was Jim. Beyond mere idolatry, I had frozen into a state of solid worship.

I rasped out that I was going home. Mere human, he moved aside. An unsettled note hung in the air, though we pretended everything was fine. I made it to my car, got inside, and watched him stroll back into the studio.

Not satisfied with merely making a fool of myself, I wanted to make it better. I left my car and went after him. I entered a room full of smoky faces and blaring music.

"Kathy's still in Palm Springs. Come by whenever you're free," I whispered.

Looking down at a sheet of words, keeping time to the music, he nodded. Reverting to my mannequin routine, I exited.

I drove home, walked straight into the bathroom, and locked the door behind me. Kneeling down across the smooth, cool tiles, I threw my arms around a hanging Turkish towel. It was soft. I grasped on as though it contained all the strength in the world; I needed it transfused through my blood to my heart. The towel became a ghost Madonna, my father's chest, my mother's skirt, God's understanding. I couldn't let go as my body filled with bitter, wracking pain. It poured through me and poured out of me; it had no end. I couldn't tell if it began inside or outside of me; the pain was all there was—and I was it.

I felt a sudden, rope-burning twist to my heart. My core was ripped apart, edges seared, wrenched open. I made unearthly sobbing noises I'd never heard. It was so involuntary, so totally physical, that I became scared of dying. After a final electric surge, the pain rippled out and left me limp. Exhausted from fighting or surrendering, I curled into a ball on the floor. My broken heart didn't feel like a poetic metaphor; it felt literal. Pulling the towel down next to me for a pillow, I fell asleep, knowing I wouldn't see Jim again for weeks . . . months . . .

My heartbreak flowed into the summer of 1969. Kathy left for Taos, New Mexico; I left for Laguna Beach. A true mecca for hippies, Laguna was teeming with brown rice, organic vegetables, pregnant earth mothers in embroidered clothes, and their old men selling psychedelics. Laguna Canyon had a whole little village, including the Brotherhood of Eternal Love, and my mother started sewing for Mystic Arts. For a while, it was a magical place. I first tasted homemade carrot cake under the canyon stars, and like the cake, there was a wholesome purity and sweetness between people. I was just too screwed up to be a hippie.

In the midst of the gentle flow around me, I wanted to laugh, cry, or scream. Wearing homespun, ethnic clothes, with no makeup and my hair hanging loose, I was accepted as a sister; but if I applied makeup, curled my hair, or ate at Taco Bell, I was a spiritual reject. I did both on purpose and grew more disillusioned. The summer passed slowly, a hot cocoon to bear until the shedding and release of fall. But it finally ended. I took off for the corrupt city, where I could be miserable in peace.

Blue Boy

I was back in L.A. for my second year of art school when
I received Jim's next 3 AM call. Not bothering to give his
name, he said, "Judy? I'm lonely." He paused as this sank
into my brain cells. "Will you come and make love with
me?" he asked.

I didn't answer. Staring into the dark, I felt dismayed
that my heart was beating so fast.

"I've come by your place, but you're never there. I
thought you'd moved or something." This avowal tipped
the scales; willpower seemed absurd.

"OK, I'll come. Where are you, anyway?" I asked.

"At the office. And I'm cold. Will you bring a blanket?"

"Uh-huh . . . it's red with a black stripe and not even
itchy."

"Are you making fun of me? Are you really going to
come?" he asked dubiously.

"I said I was. I just have to get dressed and stuff."

"Good. Remember the blanket. I'm not even drunk!"
With this declaration, he hung up.

As I dressed, Kathy sighed loudly, flopping over on
her stomach in disgust. Soon, I was driving down the
deserted streets, heart pounding through the echoing
silence. Racing the dawn, I rode to a man on the other

side: my child, lover, father, brother from antiquity. Put me on a plate, probe me with a needle, and my one and only word would have been *Jim*.

He was exuberant upon my arrival. When I pulled up, he ran outside naked, hung over the railing, and waved. Only vaguely surprised, I wondered if he'd fall.

"You're beautiful," he shouted. "Beautiful!" He seemed a bit delirious, but I liked it. "Take off your clothes. I want to see all of you!" I was an exhibitionist at heart; my long, flowing Greek goddess clothes were perfect for undressing in a parking lot.

"Oh, you're beautiful!" Jim applauded blissfully.

I did "Nude Ascending the Staircase" wonderfully. It seemed too bad it wasn't midday so we could bring entertainment back to the people on boring lunch breaks.

When I walked inside, Jim stood on the far side of the room and issued questions. "Haven't you missed me? Hasn't it been a long time?" His eyes bored into mine, his magnetism hypnotizing me. I walked trancelike across the space separating us. He wrapped his arms around me, enfolding, molding me to him. Tilting my head back, his fingers played over the contours of my face until he pulled my body strong against his, suddenly passionate. He lost himself, surrendered to the moment without trying. His sincerity blew me away, turned me to wind, silver-blue. This was the kiss all perfumes aimed for: unrepeatable, unforgettable.

But the spell broke, and another part of him came back in full-blown, X-rated soap-opera mode. We fell to the red blanket spread across the floor for a picnic. For the first piece of the morning, we were cast as lustful animals. "I'm an animal—an animal," he yelled. "Do you understand?"

"Yes." I could only imagine myself as a lion or a horse, which made it hard to relate. So I watched him.

"I'm an animal," he repeated, but the novelty wore off. He changed scenes; this was an old one, the dialogue only slightly updated. "Whose girl are you?"

"Yours," I said.

"Are you only my girl?"

"Yes."

"I own you! You're mine—only mine!" I thought this was pushing it, but he looked demonic. "I own you, don't I?"

"Yes." I sounded bored, feeling my resentment combine with fear.

Instead of making him angry, my lack of enthusiasm seemed to unnerve him. "You and me, Judy. You and me. . . ." He may have thought the romantic murmur evocative, but it was just an incomplete sentence. Getting more physical, he went down on me. "I love your pussy," he said. I figured pussies were pretty much the same and remained unmoved. "You're so beautiful!" I was really tired of that one; beauty was a shell.

"Just wait!" I spit out ferociously.

"Wait for what?" he asked.

"Wait until you see what I'm really going to be like!"

"But there's nothing to wait for. You're already beautiful," he said, staring at me like I'd lost my senses. "What's there to wait for?"

Did he think this was my goal in life—being some beautiful girl? Wait until I'm grown up! Any concept of who I really was escaped him. But Jim just looked hurt, as if I was evading him.

"Now, now, now," he repeated, drifting into a litany. Crying, he gasped, "I never want this to end. I never want it to end!" He worked himself into a frenzy; more crying, more despair, because it was going to end, and he was going to die. After coming, he assumed a dignified air of sanity and walked to the phone to call an airline. He hung up and laughed. "Well, I just missed that flight to New York." He was supposed to be at some film festival; everyone was probably thinking he'd disappeared again. Oh well . . .

Jim walked around aimlessly, chortling to himself. I tried to stand. After finding my balance, I walked to the window and looked out. I felt sad, crushed by the dreary view. He came to my side and took my hand. "Isn't love nice?" he asked.

I couldn't imagine how the words came out of his mouth. Love could kill you, and he thought it was nice? I felt like a soft bird caught in his hands, one he could mutilate with the slightest pressure. My mood wasn't particularly uplifting, and he began to look mournful. Turning from the window, he looked into my eyes. "Would you marry me?"

I noticed the "would" but hadn't the wits for guile. "Yes," I said.

"You'd really marry me?"

I affirmed it a few times. Knowing he was a person someone would marry seemed to cheer him up. He suggested we go to the other room, where we could get more comfortable.

He took my blanket, spreading it across the couch as I trailed behind. "I can't believe how much you've changed," he said. "You just used to be this funky little girl. Now you're a movie star!" I guess this was progress, but I didn't see myself as either of those characters. "I really mean it," he said.

I felt like a nice, faithful dog that panted along after her master, not exactly knowing why. I padded over to the couch, sat on the far end, and hid my body under the blanket. Jim watched that little routine. "I love you," he said.

"Oh, I know, just like a person loves their dog."

"No," he said, sounding offended. Maybe I should've explained I was a perfectly admirable, worthwhile dog. "I love you like a human being! I do," he said. I didn't see how he could love me as a human being when he didn't even know me, but I feared insulting his integrity any further. "Do you love me?" he asked, childlike.

"Yes," I said in a small voice.

"How come you never tell me then? If you really love me, you'll have to prove it by telling me a thousand times!"

"I love you, I love you, I love you, I love you." I was beginning to hope he wasn't serious. "I love you, I love . . ."

"How many men have you gone to bed with?" Jim interrupted. His tone was serious now.

"Four, counting you." I didn't know if that seemed like a lot or a little.

"Four?" he sounded astonished.

"Yeah." I probably should have said seventy-five or two hundred eleven. My image was in jeopardy.

"You're practically a virgin," he burst out, flushed. "I feel really privileged." He looked embarrassed and thrilled, like he'd just made it with the Virgin Mary. "Do you think maybe I'm too old for you?" His sin was reduced to child molestation.

"No. I think it's about right. You're only seven years older than I am. My dad's seven years older than my mom."

"I guess. What is Huddleston, anyway?" he asked.

"My last name."

"No, I mean what ancestry?"

"It's English. But my mother is French, and there's a feud over which part is Scottish or Irish." I might as well have said mongrel.

"I didn't think you were Jewish." He sounded relieved, so I gave him a dirty look. "It's just that Jewish girls are on this weird trip sometimes. I don't get along with them very well. . . . You know, I think we should go to the woods for a weekend. I know where we could go. Do you want to?"

"Yeah, I love the woods. My first backyard was a lot of woods. I always feel good there."

Jim curled up next to me, pulling the blankets over us. He mumbled about needing sleep and soon faded out, leaving me wide awake. His skin was so white and cool; I could feel its damp texture every time he breathed. Staring at the marked calendar, I drowsily computed his performance dates. This will never last, my mind warned. I worried that I'd never reach him; he'd never believe I loved him. I could go down on my knees, cry testimony to God, beg him to believe, but still he never would.

I'd drifted off for a few hours when Jim noisily awoke, good humored and ready for the day. After I dressed and was brushing my hair, he came up behind me. "You have such good taste," he said, looking awestruck. I was wearing a strapless, flowing tunic and pants. I didn't know why he found that so remarkable; Pam wasn't the only good dresser.

"Oh, don't start that ritual up again," I said.

"Don't get all huffy!" he protested. "You know, pretty soon people will be arriving. You don't want them to come in and see us all naked and crazy, do you?"

"No, not really," I said. He blithely pulled my top down to my waist, making a well-aimed below-the-waist attempt to put me in a frenzy. Having made a mess of me, he laughed. I came up for a gasp of air, gave him an evil glance, and laughed back. As I straightened my clothes, he told me about all the great movies we'd go see. I cynically wondered if this would happen before or after our trip to the woods. Still, half of me believed him—maybe even more.

It was time for me to go to art school, which seemed to impress him anew. As we walked downstairs, he looked infatuated by whoever he thought I was. When we got to my car, I turned into a statue. "You have green eyes!" he exclaimed.

"I always have," I replied coolly.

"And you even look beautiful in the morning like this!" he continued, undaunted. Then he hugged me, a big teddy-bear hug. "You're going to be my new girlfriend from now on. Huh?"

"Uhm-hmn," I agreed, taken over by his tenderness. It felt more intimate with the noisy traffic surrounding us; we seemed more alone in a poignant, lovesick sense.

"It's not just the sex. I could just go on holding you like this forever. I never want to let you go." He held me back to survey me for a second; then he pulled me close again. I smiled and slid into my car. He was saying dangerous things. Believing him scared me; I didn't want to hear his words run through my head at night when I was trying to sleep. I remained calm, watching him lean over me, a portrait of loving sincerity. "Have a good day," he said, and kissed me good-bye, his star pupil.

Sunshine of My Love

During the next month, I started suffering from a malady I called Reality Attacks. I'd be walking, talking, eating, drawing, doing anything, when an attack would strike my stomach and shoot in an adrenaline rush to my brain. Waiting for Kathy in the art-school parking lot one day, I was studying the stained pavement when my vision shifted to a car. Its massive thing-ness seemed astounding enough, but the black patch spreading across the ground in a perfect upside-down car replica was even more amazing: a shadow. Slowly, the shape transformed. My attention shifted to the sun, the real culprit. Suspended in space, we were traveling around a glowing red-orange ball of fire. It was just stuck up there, burning, causing shadows to move. The movement showed how sundials measured time. My heart raced; I could hardly breathe. How people kept plodding along with such miracles occurring daily was beyond me.

I didn't want to have a breakdown or heart attack at twenty, so I visited my old doctor in Newport. He didn't seem thrilled by my wild-haired, braless, red-shawled look and asked if I was using speed. That was almost amusing—amphetamines would spin me out forever.

After numerous tests, the doctor assured me I was fine; I was simply too high-strung.

"At your age, you should be enjoying life," he explained. "You shouldn't worry so much."

He prescribed Valium. After sampling a few, I was tranquil as can be. Even two of them turned a Reality Attack into a mere curiosity.

Driving back to Hollywood with the past fading behind and the future looming ahead, I tried to analyze what was causing my mental state. It was more than shadows and light. I'd operated under the illusion that I was unique, an artist destined to create something significant; the problem would be achieving it. The possibility that I would not, after all, marry Jim, had dawned on me. I might have to struggle alone for years, poor, ill, or deluded, trying to come up with a masterpiece. I might die alone and anonymous. There might be no mark of my existence, no art, no poetry, not even a tombstone. Everyone has to do it alone, my mind warned me in terror.

"Most women are good in art school, but when they leave, they usually just get married and make their own sculptures." The recent quote from one of my male painting teachers blared up at me. Babies. Women made babies. This consuming talent was the reason cited for the small number of famous women artists. There must be a mistake. After all, humans were prone to err. Once, people thought the world was flat and God had a beard.

In high school, I'd once prayed in the backseat of a car until I got stuck midprayer. I studied the stream of nonstop cars, each filled with people, and realized this was just one insignificant freeway in California. What if they were all praying, too? How could God listen to me? There would never be enough time; even if angels relayed messages, it wouldn't be fast enough. There would be a long waiting line—first come, first served. And what about all the people in Italy, Africa, and China? It wouldn't be possible to be heard over such international clamor to the skies. My childhood concept of God with a beard died, but God didn't. I hoped the same thing was true about women artists; I just had to find a different point of view.

The omniscient presence of a strict disciplinarian, judging and rebuking my behavior, was familiar. But God the Father is a difficult concept if you've had problems with your father. God was a man; Jesus was a man; even Buddha and Muhammad were men. Across the board, the divine was called "he," and language created reality. In high school, there was no way I could envision myself, a virgin slut on her way to hell, as good or holy. At the time, there was no feminine divine acknowledged beyond a virgin mother. If God equaled father, equaled men, then rebelling against my father and men was rebelling against God. Paradoxically, he became what I sought most illusively in love.

That night I woke to rain pouring in torrents, beating tattooed patterns across the roof. The rain stopped suddenly, and a preternatural stillness pervaded the silence. A few moments later the phone rang. Glancing at the clock, I saw it was 4 AM. So it was Jim. My body remained immobile; I had no desire to leap from the bed and grab the phone. I could see him alone, hurting, but I knew he'd make me weaker. The standard ten rings took an eternity to end. In the chill following them, I summoned up my cynicism. Now he could call the next girl on his list. . . . I fell asleep with bitterness and pain, but the next day the sun rose, and the rain was gone.

∽

The next time he called, I answered, and his voice was as sexy, sad, and coaxing as ever. My heart choked in my throat as I gave way, falling back into my old dream; this would be the time. The time for *what* was hardly clear. Underneath, I still secretly hoped we'd drift off into Utopia together. When I reached the parking lot, a sight closer to a modern version of the Inferno awaited.

Either dead or passed out, some guy's warped body had fallen from the front door of Jim's blue Mustang. Contorted like a pretzel, his lower legs were caught around the gearshift knob; his head hung a few inches above the ground. I approached slowly, wondering if I should at least fold him back up, but his noisy, upside-down breathing unnerved me. I tiptoed past.

Inside, Jim didn't look much better than his friend, but he was at least sitting. Slumping, actually, while writing directly on the desk. He scribbled for a few moments, not reacting, or perhaps oblivious, to my presence. I stared at a beige candle shaped like a cock and noticed no one had lit it yet. Judging from his ghastly white face and bleary eyes, Jim wasn't exactly with it.

"Can we go to your house?" His voice rasped. "Please? I hate it here! And I don't want to go to any motels." A shudder of loathing passed through him. "Won't you take me to your house?" My house seemed to have turned into the Utopia I couldn't find.

"Sure, come on," I said, hoping he could make it downstairs. "Your friend . . . he looks kind of sick down there."

"Babe can take care of himself. He's just fine. Leave him alone," Jim snarled, throwing me a suspicious glare.

"OK, I just felt sorry for him," I said, taken aback.

Flouncing around the room, he indignantly picked up the belongings he'd scattered. "Can we go now?" he asked impatiently.

"Yes."

"I'm so glad we can go to a house!" He babbled behind me in incoherent spurts as we walked to my car. On the ride there, he lapsed into silence, and he seemed half-asleep when we reached my place. He followed me inside, and we marched past Kathy to the rear bedroom. We used the large room as a studio, and it was crammed with wall-to-wall paintings and a rickety cot for emergencies. Jim, the endless emergency, fell across it as if it were a silken divan. He looked around in confusion but became calm as I undressed him and covered him with sheets. A pleased look settled over his face as I tucked the blankets in.

"Aren't you going to lay down with me?" he asked, looking alarmed.

"Just a second," I said. I couldn't imagine where I'd fit but took off my clothes anyway. Abnormally cooperative, he helped me find a comfortable position beside him.

"Won't you talk to me? Just say anything you want. Flow of consciousness, you know, anything that comes to your mind. Just talk to me," he said.

"Nothing comes to my mind, and I don't know what to . . ."

"Golden. Golden—you're golden!" Jim's eyes grew wider, taking in my goldenness. I was relieved I wouldn't have to talk. He wove my hair around his fingers as he repeated his transfixed vision. "Golden, golden . . ."

"What is this?" he asked, pointing to his cock.

"I don't know," I said, stupefied. Looking obsessed by the strange attachment to his body, Jim regarded it abstractly.

"What is it?" he asked in a four-year-old's voice. He was playing around like my first-grade boyfriend. Sensual curiosity, not only sexual. It was kind of fun.

"It's real obvious looking. Primeval," I offered. "Like an ancient mushroom."

Jim pulled me down next to him, rocking me back and forth in a slow, reassuring motion. It seemed oddly comforting in the confines of the small space. I couldn't tell who was the parent or the child anymore; it was all a pleasant blur. "I love you," he said, burying his head between my breasts. "I love you, I love you," he repeated in a tiny, touching voice of belief and need. He repeated his words and continued his slight rocking until he fell asleep to the fairy-tale lullaby. I went with him.

When we woke later, light streamed through the windows. I walked around and picked up clothes while Jim watched, mildly dazed. "We've always had an understanding, haven't we?" he asked, his expression sweet and hopeful.

"I think I've always understood you . . . I don't think you understand me," I said, hurt that he hadn't said a word about my paintings—which were literally lining the room. My remark hung in the air, floated somewhere over his head. He looked disappointed, but it didn't occur to me to directly say it was my work, my soul he was ignoring.

Kathy had gone, and we went back to my bed, where we could be noisy without worry. He was Jim the man now, no longer the child. All traces of drunkenness had disappeared. A bit of the previous, trusting magic drifted between us, though his sensuality had been transfused with plain sex. The only thing that seemed spectacular or unusual was that it wasn't spectacular or unusual. We fell asleep again.

When we woke up, Jim inspected the stack of books by my bed. "Are all these for school?" he asked, sounding amazed.

"No, none of them are. They're for me," I said. I'd been a bookworm since childhood and felt upset he didn't have that basic fact.

Discovering a William Blake book, he quoted random blurbs from memory. "I really love Blake! He's one of my favorite writers," he said. "Can I borrow this for a little while? I'm always meaning to go to Pickwick and get it, but I just never get around to it." He was so excited that I said he could keep it. I'd run out and get another one; Blake soothed Reality Attacks as well as Valium did. For now, our affinity for Blake softened the mood as we dressed for our separate worlds.

"All good things must come to an end," he said, pausing at the front door. He flashed me a hopeless smile to make up for the corny phrase. I wanted to drag him back into my world, beg him never to leave, plead that things didn't have to end. But I didn't. The door closed and I locked it. We walked to my car, the heads of a funeral procession.

"You look radiant. You look like you're in love," Jim said in the car. He sounded shocked and kept his eyes on my face. The words echoed over to me; I thought they implied I was in love with someone else, not him. Stung to the quick, I stared straight ahead.

"Maybe it's your makeup . . . you've changed your makeup. You hardly wear any."

"No." I shook my head, half smiling in confusion.

"It must be that all you wear is mascara now." He dug fruitlessly for the cause of my damn radiance, which must have vanished by then. If someone created mascara that produced love radiance, that person would make millions.

"I guess I just feel better about things. So maybe I look better." I shrugged, lying for survival.

"I wish I could mellow out. . . . I keep thinking I'll have to. Maybe someday I'll have peace of mind." His voice was hollow with longing. Despite myself, despite the fact that he didn't know love when it was staring him in the face, I felt for him again.

"I just hope I don't get some long disease like cancer." Jim rolled his eyes upward. "Spare me from cancer!" He brooded a moment; then he looked cautiously at me. "Sometimes I call you because I'm afraid I'm going to die alone." He paused. "I want someone to write down the things I say while I'm dying." I nodded.

Suddenly, we were parked in front of the office. We sat there, saying nothing, looking at the parking lot. There was a sad, unfinished feeling in the air. He reached over and hugged me; then he sat back, searching my eyes, as if whatever was missing lay inside them. Jim was looking for confirmation, too, but I couldn't acknowledge it. My stubborn ego, my hurt pride—I couldn't say, "I love you." After our long, baffled pause, he got out of the car. He stood there, looking awkward and unsure. "Good-bye," he said. "I'll call you tonight." Jim regained his aura of cool control and walked away. He remembered who he was, why he was there. As if from his vision, I saw myself: the girl in the car, fading away. I could feel him watching me and had to look again. He caught me in his eyes, faltering and lost for another moment. I managed to semi-smile, semi-wave a semi-good-bye. I had to leave before I lost my mind.

Not to Touch the Earth

One rainy night, after painting a land of glass castles guarded by misty, swaying vines and opalescent-eyed women, I donned my purple velvet dress. Imagining people who danced liquidly through forests, I floated barefoot into the rain and got in my car. Under the spell I'd cast, I felt like a magical new creature, and I had to tell Jim I loved him before the trance wore off. I drove down the wet, neon streets, reflective washes of rain illuminating and soothing the fraying edges of my mind.

When I reached the office, his car was in the parking lot. I leapt out—a rabbit into pure space. When I touched the ground, my eyes fell upon a girl in a long dress. She had such a strange, stately quality that it seemed I should run up and hug her, like a long-lost relative. I restrained myself; this was a stranger in a parking lot. She smiled as I approached. "Where's Jim?" I asked.

"Away." The syllables were elongated and dramatic; her nearly emaciated arms moved fluidly through the air, demonstrating his away-ness. Giving me a concerned look, she said, "You need some water! You should see yourself—the way you just flew out of your car, you might never land." She laughed.

I smiled uncertainly.

"I'm Jim's sister. It's lucky I'm here to help you! I'll take you over to the Clear Thoughts Building; it has good water." She laughed again, as if to reassure me. "You're going much too fast. Come on."

"I guess it's true," I said, laughing halfheartedly. I didn't really want to go there. I'd have to see Themis, the boutique Jim bought for Pam. I preferred ignoring the bond it represented. But taken in by the girl's desire to cure me with water, I figured I could risk it; maybe she really was Jim's sister. She looked me up and down, nodding approval at my bare feet.

"You should always go barefoot in the city," she said, also shoeless. "You have to keep in contact with yourself and the ground."

"It's cement," I said.

"Well, usually. But whenever you see real ground, walk on it instead."

"People don't like that," I said, referring both to the ground and bare feet.

"That doesn't matter." We had reached the drinking fountain unharmed, and she monitored my water drinking. "Everything's based on water. We come from the sea. It works better than any drug. It'll always cure you—not like other things. You really have to calm down. You're almost panting!"

"I know," I said, sneaking two yellow Valium into my mouth.

"Jim and I are the illegitimate children of Ingrid Bergman and Orson Welles," she confided in a secretive, lowered tone. I arranged my face properly. "We were separated when we were very young. It was a scandal because we were always trying to make love!"

"Oh, really?" I tried to sound unalarmed. This was getting a bit more elaborate than I'd expected.

"Yes, but sometimes Jim forgets. It was such a long time ago." She smiled gently and nodded. "You'd better drink some more water; you need a lot."

"Uh-huh," I agreed, gulping mouthfuls. Maybe it would work.

"Now that I've returned to my rightful place," she continued, "we'll get married. But first, we have to solve the incest law. People have this legal thing about incest. It's so ridiculous. We love each other, but they don't want us to get married."

"My girlfriend really loved her brother, too," I said, feeling I should offer something. "It was kind of weird, only he was just a stepbrother. I guess that's different. . . . What about Pam?" I asked quickly, so it wouldn't seem important.

"Oh, Pam." She waved her away, too. "Pam and Jim helped each other through a lot of hard times when they didn't have anyone to love. But that's over now. Pam's in love with Ned, the co-owner of Themis, anyway."

"I thought she was devoted to Jim," I said, my image of their relationship crumbling.

"No. It was just security for both of them," she said dismissively. "What do they call you?"

"Judy."

"I'm Joanna."

Back at the office, she insisted we sit down in the muddy little garden instead of going upstairs. Secretly hoping that Jim was up there and would hear our voices, I crouched down beside her. "The earth people are trying to take us over. We have to be very careful," she said.

"That's true," I sighed. They had certainly been trying to take me over for years.

"I spotted you as a water person right away. They aren't many left, you know. They look like ancient, aristocratic statues. We both look that way; have you noticed?" In the half-light, our faces did bear a resemblance.

"It's funny they don't recognize us," I said, wondering if insanity was catching.

"They will." She explained her oddly formulated views, a mix of world mythologies turned into her own reality. We laughed about the lemmings that never drowned and earth people obsessed with serious living. She was bright to have created such a strange brew, but the light breeziness had begun to drag. "Soon, our place as leaders will be given back to us. We have the true origins of life behind us. We'll start a new race."

"How?"

"It'll start when Jim and I are married and walk into the sea. Others will follow. The people who aren't afraid, who believe. . . . Do you know that Jim loves me so much, he said he would sacrifice his bridge for me?" This, I assumed, was her name for his male genitals.

"Jim said that?" It was impossible to believe Jim would do such a thing for anyone, even if his life depended on it. I still felt a twinge of jealousy as my doubt about her grew.

"But he has so much trouble remembering our past. He's so attached to being an earth person! You wouldn't think so, would you?" She paused unhappily.

"Not really," I said.

"His parents—the ones that took him after we split up—didn't love him. I asked how much his father loved him, and he made a little space between his thumb and forefinger." She illustrated the gesture. "I asked how much his mother loved him, and he . . ." She widened the gap a bit more. "Isn't that sad? He couldn't even talk about it!"

I sensed her compassion, and this story sounded sad but true. Yet I felt tired and overexposed, like a piece of film left to burn in the sun. "It's too bad you don't have a soul mate, too," she said. "It's too bad Brian Jones is dead; he would've been perfect for you. Maybe Charlie Watts—you have the same lionish coloring."

I shook my head no. If she'd taken Jim and was about to castrate and drown him, at least she could wave her wand at Mick Jagger. She'd been interesting, but I wanted to go.

"I have this crazy ex-lover. He's been following me all across the country since I was released from the institution." She stopped and looked angry, like she sensed my withdrawal. "You know, I knew a girl there just like you. She didn't have a soul mate either, but at least she made sense. . . . Anyway, he won't stop following me. He's staying across the street so he can watch me."

"He's across the street?" I squirmed, glancing toward the Tropicana motel.

"Yes." She sounded off-hand about it. "He says he's going to assassinate Jim and then me. He's so jealous—he won't give up. You'd better be careful, though; he may mistake you for one of us and hit you."

"Yeah, well, I'd better go then . . ." I stood up, worried about getting shot, and clutched my car keys. The girl called Joanna didn't react, too busy looking around for her ex. I said good-bye and drove back to my stodgy reality feeling stupid and clumsy, a regular earth person. I envied her freedom, her fleeting mania; she was really onto something—just a little too on for me. It was seductive, but I wasn't yet ready for the sea.

Shaman's Blues

After my fleeting acquaintance with the edge, I took a few steps back. It was 1970; falling off that edge looked too easy for comfort, and there seemed to be drawbacks. Sometimes the line between reality and perception—between what I saw and what I merely sensed—became diffuse. Defining these borders made me uneasy; sometimes it was difficult to trust myself. I wasn't as crazy as Joanna, but sometimes I wanted to be. More often, I was scared of being deluded. Wasn't I the one who believed Jim was my soul mate? Wasn't I just another one of those crazy girls? And there were so many of them. I tried not to think about it—just as I'd tried not to notice the smog. Then it was all I saw. It might have been wiser to make a plea for sanity.

But when Jim called the next time, I was still crazy enough to accept the request to rescue him from deathly solitude. When I arrived, he jumped into the car in a panic. He wanted me to take him to the Alta Cieñega Motel—only half a block away—but I guessed he couldn't go alone. I hadn't been there since the beginning.

It was rush hour, and La Cieñega was overflowing with traffic. Under Jim's influence, I made an illegal left-hand turn. Nearly crashing into us, a harried blonde woman honked, screamed inarticulately, and waved her arms. Jim smiled politely at her. Then he turned to me, grinning with wisdom. "Pretend your car is broken," he said.

Laughing, I turned into the driveway. It was still too steep. Walking upstairs to his room brought on a mild Reality Attack from remembering the first times we were together. Jim stopped and turned around to me. "Oh, you've never been here with me. Have you?" he asked innocently. Stricken, I couldn't answer, unsure if he was serious or taunting me. Breathing could be difficult if you weren't a compassionate woman who laughed at the stupid things he did.

Once inside, he was somber. "I met this guy last night. He wants me to act in a film he's making," he said.

"What's it about?"

"There's this band of wild, hashish-smoking children wandering around in a Moroccan dessert. I would lead them."

"Oh," I said diplomatically. It sounded pretty weird to me. "I think you ought to be careful about what you're in."

"This guy seemed pretty together," he said, shaking his head defensively. "I want to get more involved with film somehow. I'd like to write some screenplays."

"Yeah, I like the way you write, only"—the words spilled out of me—"why's it always so morbid?"

"I write about sex and death. And if you think that's morbid, well . . ." He shot me an icy look.

"But, that one line—about pulling your eyes out."

"That's about a contemporary issue. Smog," he explained.

"I like the part about being metamorphosed from a mad dancing body on the hillside to . . ."

"To a pair of eyes staring in the dark," he finished for me.

"I had to tear out your dedication. 'To Pamela Susan,' " I confessed. "I even made a collage out of it . . . something about fallen birds glazed with ink stains."

"I felt I owed it to her." Ever the diplomat, he minimized his bonds, showing no particular allegiance.

"I went into her shop one day. It was nice," I said noncommittally. My penchant for confession was going too far. Her dress shop, Themis, had seemed more of an opulent environment than a regular boutique—high-end hippie with a Moroccan vibe. Pam had breezed over, noticed the Japanese silk dress I was wearing, and clutched at the material, her huge green eyes hypnotized. Wearing an embroidered robe top and pants, she seemed slightly giddy.

"You just never see fabric like this anymore. It's so beautiful!" she'd said, forgetting to let go of the silk and staring at me. Her pale, freckled face was beautiful, like a tiny cameo.

"It was from a kimono my dad got during the war," I said. "In Japan . . ."

Kathy, sensing a meltdown, had found a quick excuse for us to exit the shop. She assured me Pam was just stoned; it had nothing to do with remembering my face. It had been nearly four years since we split her last piece of gum backstage.

"I don't think she knows who you are." Jim offered this profound synopsis from his pillow on the bed. "Pam's a good nest builder," he explained. "She's a Capricorn." Apparently that summed her up, though I didn't know what he meant. "She's just so vulnerable about everything." His complaining voice rose a notch.

"I thought vulnerability was good. I mean, at least you feel." I wanted to defend her; at the same time, I hoped he'd put her down.

"No, she's too vulnerable. There's a difference," he said. "Besides, we're both egomaniacs. It can never work out." I couldn't think of any intelligent quips on egomania and just sat there, feeling too absorbent, a big soppy mess, listening. "I'm usually with older women, anyway."

"Are they really that different? All the women?" I asked. "It seems like it'd get boring or something."

"Yeah. They're all pretty much the same. I don't know why I do it." He sighed, his voice full of heavy dejection. "You know, I think we're all slaves to our bodies!" Jim pronounced, glancing around tensely. "I say 'you know' too often. I can't stand it when other people do it! I wish I'd stop."

"I have some Valium with me. Maybe we should take some and just relax," I said.

"Really? I like Valium."

"Yeah," I said. "I probably have a lifelong prescription for them. I get these alienated feelings that nothing is real, so I have to take them."

"Oh, that's a bad one." He looked wary, as if I'd admitted a contagious disease. Grabbing four blue pills from my hand, he swallowed them down, erasers for lashing minds. "There was this young girl once. . . . I was with her one night in Hawaii. We didn't talk or anything. But it was just so refreshing, like a spring bath. . . . I'll never forget it. I don't even know who she was."

"I met another girl you knew—Joanna, I think her name was. She was sort of crazy." I realized she could actually be his sister and cut any further comments.

"Sort of crazy? She was really crazy! Not even good crazy."

"She was all right for a night," I shrugged.

"No. I was afraid she'd do something to me." He flinched.

"Oh, yeah. Maybe so." I recalled her remark about sacrificing his bridge.

"You know, I just discovered that men and women are really different." Jim spoke as if this was of vital importance. "I'd always assumed they were alike, men and women. But they aren't. We don't even see things the same!" He turned anxiously toward me, his face a ruined jigsaw puzzle. "What do you think about that?"

"I'm not really sure. I can see it both ways."

After my noncommittal answer, his face appeared even more confused. If he was having an identity crisis over gender, I didn't want to tell him he was the most female male I'd known.

"Well, I guess there has to be some difference. Otherwise there'd be just one sex instead of two," I assured him. I giggled at the words and the slurred, loose way they fell out. The Valium was taking effect, the tenseness of life easing.

"You know," Jim drawled, "we've known each other for three-and-a-half years now!"

"That's true," I mumbled, pleased. I'd never figured this out, so the extra half a year seemed particularly astute—he'd computed it exactly. If he could do that, he must have remembered the times I'd been there before. He reached for me, and we were two flesh-and-blood beings making love without theatrics. It was real. Isolated in a nondescript motel room, with cars honking and ambulances scream-ing, we were alive together. Humans being. Poignancy lin-gered, acid, raw, undisguised, admitting things never said but always known. In fleeting grace, our identities were gone; love surfaced, brave, scared, and untarnished. In a world of fucking, fucking with clothed souls and masked cores, that naked love seemed the ultimate hope and para-noia. We were stripped clean to the bone.

After lying in the aftermath of the unknown, we took a shower. Getting back in the bed, he turned on an old Cary Grant movie. We collapsed in histrionics; the characters seemed crazed with unfounded jealousy and accusations. "They just don't know about cosmic consciousness!" Jim snorted gleefully. "But this is a very sophisticated comedy, you know?"

"Yeah . . . but are you married or not? Lately every-one tells me you're married. They think I'm really dumb," I confessed. Friends of friends gave unsolicited reports: he'd needed her; she rushed to him. They broke up again; she had "round heels"; they'd married.

"Those people don't know what they're talking about," he said scornfully. "You just have to ignore them. I'm much too young and irresponsible to get married!"

We erased the world, words, movies, lies, and truths a little longer. Eventually Jim decided it was time to get dressed and go to work. He said he knew a good place we could have breakfast first. As I dressed, Jim sat and watched me.

"You're really big, you know?"

"Big? What do you mean, big? Do you mean fat?"

"No. I just mean big. Like Ursula Andress or Britt Eklund. That kind of big."

"Oh, OK." My ego was almost soothed.

"You ought to be a model; you'd really be a good one," he said. Hearing that, my muscles tensed in fury. Here I was, not fat, but worse, typecast as the Body.

"But I want to be an artist!" I nearly screamed.

"Do men in the street always whistle at you?" he asked.

"Only the idiots!" I retorted, turning from him as he opened the door.

Jim ignored this, too. He started whistling some stupid tune to himself. He kept it up as we walked outside and downstairs. An awkward, off-balance quality lurked between us now. It was too late to retrace my steps or ask to do that last scene over. "I'm not really hungry anymore," Jim said when we reached my car. "I think I'll just walk across the street now. Is that all right?"

"Yeah, I'm not that hungry, either," I said.

"I love you," he said over the car roof.

"I love you, too." I echoed over the tin. It sounded hollow. I walked over to his side; he looked hard and solemn. I was quiet, trying to fathom the play of his features.

"I called you a week or so ago. It was in the afternoon, so I guess you were at school. Your mother or someone answered." He sounded hesitant.

"Yeah, it was my mother. She was visiting."

"Well, she asked if you should call me at the studio. Who was she talking about? Do you know someone who has a studio? She must've thought I was someone else— some artist with a studio." He ended lamely, the sentence dead in the air, and looked at me strangely.

Fumbling with his way of turning situations backward, I tried to explain it was just semantics. Office and studio meant the same thing to her. But I couldn't bridge our gap and sensed he wasn't listening, anyway. He nodded and smiled.

"I'll call you," Jim said. My heart sank . . . those dread words. Please don't drag it into the mud of promises, I thought. When you call again, I'll come. But let's drop it with the tomorrows. It would be weeks, months; I knew that now. I smiled back at him; maybe I was finally learning. I drove away.

A few moments later, waiting at the traffic signal, I saw Jim. This man with such apparent self-confidence took his show so seriously; it meant everything, especially if he fell. He died a little each time he fell, and he fell too hard and fast. His shell looked more brittle as his insides hurt more and he believed less. From a distance, watching the way Jim walked alone, the full impact of his aloneness hit me. The man was solitary. Forever solitary.

Blonde in the Bleachers

You say Jim was solitary," Dr. Atkins said. "What about you?

"I guess I was, too . . . I mean, being an only child, you get used to it," I said.

But you don't get used to aloneness. At some point during puberty, I became defined by how I was perceived. My self was projected onto my appearance—it was all I was—and I depended on the reactions of others to know who that was. It seems beyond narcissistic, existing only in that mirrored reflection. We remained like teenagers, walking around with mirrors in front of ourselves, judging each other by the reflections, trying to find the truth of our buried selves in the process. When I'd moved to L.A., it still seemed like high school. It was as if the culture embodied by gangly, gauche California was still in adolescence: *Can you see me? Can you see me now?*

It made sense that I'd later work as a fashion model because of the carefully controlled persona such a career offered. Internally, I might have been an emotional wreck, but I saved face by presenting myself as normal—or, ironically, as a model of what a female should be. In a way, it offered a form of invisibility. I could become an image, project a socially acceptable self, and feel sheltered in an odd kind of anonymity.

My fragile surface defined relationships until it simply broke, like it did that time on the office staircase, scaring Jim and me with my suddenly unmasked fear, dependency, anger, and other, apparently endless flaws. That meltdown had cracked my surface and broken my heart. I'd shown him I cared too much, revealed that I'd wondered where he went, what he did, whom he was with. It was like blowing it in high school, but worse. Not only was I jealous, possessive, and needy, but I'd been rejected for it. I'd unwittingly exposed my most unacceptable, froglike self, and he'd just walked away. And then to follow him into the studio! I was a fool, he didn't love me, wouldn't love me, and I couldn't take back my display of raw worship. I'd never do that again. But it was more. It was forever. No one would ever love me. That was solitary.

"What about love?" Dr. Atkins asked.

"It seems like we're in shells, putting all our stories on each other. But we're born alone and we die alone."

"Do you really believe that?"

"I don't know . . . I don't know what love is anymore. I guess I never did."

In the hospital I slowed down enough to remember things. Once, I was little, and my parents took care of me. They washed my white pillowcases and gave me ginger ale when I was sick. They wanted me to be fed and clothed, to grow up with ten fingers and ten toes, to look out the window with them, to watch the wind in the pines, and to hear the sounds of music. Perhaps we all wanted it to stay that way: me so little and protected, their model child sandwiched between the two of them, forever. It was me who had to go, to grow up, though I knew they didn't want me to. Oh, the mess, the gory, complicated mess we made of love. But still I was there, still I breathed.

From my room, I could recall how sun streamed through the window of my parents' bedroom in La Cañada. Late one afternoon, Dad and I played jacks on the floor while Mom put on makeup at her dressing table. I loved watching his large hands scoop up all twelve jacks at once. We were going out for dinner at a Mexican restaurant. Fifteen minutes before, we'd all laid down for a nap on the bed. I'd watched their chests very carefully. In and out, in and out, the breath connected. Maybe her chest didn't rise at exactly the same time; maybe he was breathing in a little before she breathed out. But close enough. I held my breath, stopped to coordinate the intake and outtake to fit theirs, finding my place midflow. Our breath was a magic cord uniting us, connecting us to the ebb and flow of life, to the whole universe that came right down to the pine trees outside our window.

We were like one creature, one being, breathing together. Even our hearts beat together. I could feel my heart pounding in my throat, in my chest, and I could see the blue vein throbbing on my dad's neck, my mom's chest gently rising—pound, pound, pounding like ocean tides, the rhythm of blood flowing between us heartbeat to heartbeat. They were so beautiful, so perfect: their hands and fingers, their noses, teeth, and hair. And they knew how to do things just right—simply by using my dad's long arms, my mom's perfect legs. Their very solidness, their flesh, was what I loved. The way they dressed and laughed and talked. Once, they were gods, and they loved me. Between them, I was protected; I belonged, forever. It was all I ever wanted.

"You said that Jim never seemed to recognize you," Dr. Atkins said. "I'm wondering if you'd had that feeling before . . ."

"It seems like no one recognized me. My parents were opposites. He was a Republican; she was a Democrat. He was an introvert; she was an extrovert. I thought I was supposed to be the perfect in-between."

"You were like the meat in their sandwich—when they could no longer agree about you, the whole sandwich fell apart. It seemed unusual that your appearance was so well kept up when you were admitted. People usually let the surface go first, but yours seemed controlled."

"But I've always been that way. My mom jokes that I have a good façade. When I feel crazy inside, I need to look normal on the outside. Is that wrong?"

"Not wrong. It's only a problem if you do it so well—then no one ever knows you."

L.A. Woman

Another summer passed. In early October 1970, Jim's voice on the end of the line sounded broken and thick. "I just got back from Miami," he said. "Won't you come and see me?"

"Where are you?" I asked, unable to think clearly.

"Uh, it's the Gene Autry Hotel. You know, the big one near the corner of Sunset. . . . You'll see it—it's there."

"What room?" I scribbled down the number on a box of new slides of my paintings. "OK, I'll see you in a while."

"Wear something long and flowing, so you look like part of the procession," he said. His last command sunk in as I hung up the phone.

I asked an attendant at the gas station on Sunset if he'd heard of a Gene Autry Hotel. It was early in the morning to be getting such questions, but he smiled amiably. "It must be the Continental Hyatt House—just down the street. I think that used to be Gene Autry's," he said. I thanked the guy and drove off. The hot, dead air had a brownish-gray overcoat of leftover smoke and smog. The consuming blaze of yet another fire left a world of ash and a palpable atmosphere of bleak destruction. It looked like L.A. was finally coming to an end. When I arrived, the Hyatt House looked starkly sinister in the smudged morning twilight. A somber uniformed man placed a ticket in my hand and drove my car away.

I walked inside. A complex elevator confronted me with unfathomable colored buttons in meticulous lines; I was supposed to push one. I could barely get out of foreign cars or open modern refrigerator doors, but I choose a colored button, listened to the jolt, and entered an elevator. I'd mastered another feat. Arriving intact on the right floor, I knocked on his hotel room door. He opened it a suspicious crack, deemed me safe, and let me in.

Jim stood on the other side, naked as usual, looking tragic as hell. I must've forgotten—that was Jim. His face was totally drained of feeling. I glanced around his hollow suite: sterile luxury filled only by two quarts of vodka, one almost empty, sitting side by side, next to some white powder, a telephone, and some orange juice.

"I just got back from Miami," he said, as if it was his explanation for being.

"Was it awful?" I didn't know many details about his trial in Miami; I just knew he and the law couldn't possibly mix. "I mean, all the legal games . . . money for freedom . . ." I trailed off as his face closed down and he made a dismissive gesture, ending further discussion. Fearful that the sullen atmosphere would take solid shape and attack me, I sat on the edge of the bed and smiled tentatively. Looking at his face, I felt his beauty hit me. I slid off my sandals, and his expression softened into amiability.

"Make yourself at home," he said, a bit too suggestively. But I took off the rest of my clothes, and relief spread fully across his features. A smile appeared. I knew he wanted dreams, gentle lies; he wanted to forget. He brought over the bag of coke, and we snorted some.

"Do you want a drink?" he asked.

"No thanks, not now."

"Let's go outside, OK?"

"Yeah, all right," I said.

The wonders of cocaine soothed us both. We walked outside on the balcony, wordless and serene. Leaning out over the railing, we were naked, feeling pure and innocent, washed clean. We watched the deluge of honking cars driving through the tainted brown air of Sunset Boulevard below. Ashes fell from the sky, enveloping all the people in smoke and smog. I leaned back, suddenly unable to take the view, and his arms softly surrounded me. We're children; God, save us, I thought. Crying silently, I turned to Jim, for his eyes, sweet and kind, the harsh cruelty lost. He held me back, a glass figurine, a fragile figment of imagination.

"You're beautiful," he whispered.

"You are, too," I said, swirling and rising as he kissed me in the crystalline nether land. For this moment, the world was good. Transformed, his arm around me, protecting us both, we walked back into the room. Lying on the bed, feeling his warmth, slow euphoria rose. The feeling took us away, only to lose hold, give way, and crash us back down. Way down. Jim had lost it; he couldn't get it up. Startled, I opened my eyes and focused on his face in confusion.

"Let's have some more coke," he said. "At least it'll numb our nostrils." As he crossed the room, I looked at his body, a body once molded with such delicate beauty, whole and fine. It was wearing down, too. Maybe it would be easier to accept on a less well-made, graceless breed, but he seemed a carelessly neglected thoroughbred.

"Jim, your stomach—it's getting out of proportion to the rest of your body," I said.

"Please, don't say those terrible things to me! Are you going to do that again?" He looked frightened, wounded, and hostile.

"I've never said any terrible things to you. Stop being such a martyr—you're really getting into the tragic hero trip." My words rang back, hard and unmerciful; I looked down.

"Promise you'll never say any more bad things to me," he pleaded.

"I promise," I said, wondering what else I could say. The phone rang, interrupting whatever unkindness I might utter next. It was someone who apparently couldn't stop talking. Getting bored and angry, I glared at him. He responded by handing me the phone and putting his finger to his lips. I listened to a girl's breathless rampage.

"I have a job here—I can't leave," she said. "What am I supposed to do? I live here, and I have to work. I can't just leave! Jim?" Panicked, I handed the phone to him.

"Uh-huh, yeah," he said, handing it back to me again. The originality of listening to one of his hysterical girlfriends had worn off. I threw the phone back at him and stalked across the room to glare unimpeded. This finished the conversation for him, too. He hung up and walked over to me, appearing mildly pleased with himself.

"What was she like?" I asked impassively.

"She has long red hair. Straight down her back." He kissed my neck, his explanation stinging with brutality. I jerked away and sat down.

"Are you married or not? I don't care anymore. I just get sick of being contradicted. Everyone that thinks they know you or Pam insists you're married. I'm not kidding."

"Pam is just this crazy girl I went with once. Now she thinks we're married." Waving it off, he shrugged. "But you take even the most mystical chick and mention marriage . . ." His point trailed off, leaving the dubious effect of marriage on even the most mystical chick spread across his dismayed face. He was getting good at dismissing everyone, getting down to the fine bone of killing.

"Do you want to look at slides of my paintings?" I asked.

"Yeah, let me see them," he said, picking one up.

"Well, you have to hold them up to the light," I said.

He crossed the room and sat by a lamp. This didn't appear to help his mind to focus; when he reached the painting I'd done more under his influence than mine, he didn't even notice. Anyone could see the similarity. Warm and cool shades of muted yellow blocked out a highway leading to a desert horizon. Where the moon met the highway's edge, stretched like a shoreline, I'd painted a row of symbols: fish skeletons, spirals, sun signs, parts of an ancient language. I was stunned and hurt when he passed it by without a word.

"Don't look at any more of those! You can't see them," I said, angrily grabbing the slide box. "I want a drink." He looked puzzled and handed me some vodka and orange juice. I gulped it like soda pop. "Can I have another, please?" I asked, morosely as possible.

"I'm out of orange juice. I could send out for some. I should have some."

"Straight."

"OK." Jim shrugged, giving me an odd glance. He'd never seen my self-destructive powers unleashed. All I wanted was to get drunk and snort as much coke as possible. In his violent boredom, Jim pissed in an empty vodka bottle. He did it idly, looking on abstracted. Equally bored, I watched. Moments later, he made another wild attempt to fuck me. It didn't work again. This time I didn't feel like understanding.

"Is there something wrong with me?" I asked. "Am I doing something wrong?"

"I already feel bad enough! Don't make me feel worse!" Jim's bluesy whine was upstaged by his hostility.

"All right!" I pounced off the bed, grabbed the vodka bottle, and locked myself in the bathroom. Drinking, I studied myself in the mirror. I was definitely not repulsive, I decided; there was something wrong with him. After an adequate sulking period, I walked out, drunker, dumber, and more defiant.

"Will you put on your sandals and walk around the room?" Jim asked.

"I guess so," I said begrudgingly. It sounded pretty stupid, but there was nothing else to do. Only when I stood, I realized it was a plot to make me look like a poster for horny men. My face set haughtily as I followed his directions: an audition for walking, performed in front of a maniac.

"Stand on that chair!" he ordered. The harsh note in his voice caused a prickle of fear, mingled with the knowledge that we'd engaged in an ugly ego battle. I obeyed as snottily as possible. I stood on the chair, leaning one hip out in contempt at both our roles, and stared unflinchingly into his eyes. "Turn around!" he snarled. I turned. "Bend over!"

Summoning up my full coordination, I slipped off both my sandals and threw them at him. "I hate you!" I spit out. There could be no mistake in my pronunciation. But it had no effect. Stepping down from the chair, I flung myself violently across the bed and looked away. There was nothing, just silence.

"Well, now what're we going to do?" I asked, my voice full of disdain.

"Play Monopoly," he hissed back.

I buried my head under a pillow, wanting to burrow away. The phone rang again. Through the muffled cotton, I heard him say, "Call back later. I'm asleep." He must have been making a stack of friends. He made another call, asked for a room number, and had a conversation about the absurdity of weddings with his friend Babe, the human pretzel who had passed out midfall from Jim's car. They had a pretty slick Vaudeville phone routine down; when they hung up, Jim seemed revived. He offered me more cocaine.

"I could take this," he said, holding up his leather belt, "and just sort of flick you on the ass with it."

"I don't like pain," I said, taking another hit of cocaine.

"It doesn't hurt. It just sensitizes your nerve endings. I wouldn't do it hard."

"I'm not some kind of physical masochist!"

"You mean you won't even try it?" he asked, taunting me.

"OK, but you'd better not hurt me."

He made three light flicks over my body. It didn't hurt, but it didn't do a thing for my nerve endings, either. Aside from that, I didn't like the look in his eyes.

"I think it's boring," I said, slowly turning over. "I mean, unless you're really into pain and being whipped, it just isn't interesting." Jim looked disappointed and sat down to pout with his useless belt.

Moments later, his other redhead called again. Persistent girl, I thought; she can have him, complete with stage directions and belts. . . . I could only guess her words from his.

"I don't know," he said. "I don't know what will happen. They haven't decided. Do you love me? When I'm in jail, you can bring me chocolate chip cookies, and I'll write all the time. It won't be bad . . ." I guessed he thought he was Oscar Wilde now. Irritated, I walked away to put on my clothes. Watching me dress, Jim caught my attention with an upraised hand.

"I love you," he said to her. Then, sure he was holding my eyes, he winked. Winked . . . like we were partners in crime. Winked like he did the first night. I thought how easily it could be me on that phone line. He didn't love anyone, just like he didn't believe anyone loved him. I had to get the hell away, leave behind the years I'd lost dreaming about him. Decisively, I reached for my purse, smoothed down my clothes and hair.

Jim hung up. His eyes full of nothing but anguish, Jim's how-could-you-leave-now expression brought on a strong, angry reaction. Surging, I felt evil. I slipped down to his side, caressed and kissed his head; then I moved down for a full-scale attack on his body. Moaning softly, acting overcome with lust, I did everything I knew to make him lose control. I wanted to make him come—to have that final power over him. I hated him. This was the only way I knew to win: take over his impotence, his drinking, women, lies, and bullshit, force him to drop the pain he held against him like a sacred shield. When he came inside me, I had a moment of Pyrrhic victory. It didn't last.

My plan of leaving immediately afterward backfired. An unearthly cry came tearing out of me. I sat up with a jagged, brutal movement and pushed him away.

"I hate you, I hate you." I was half crying, half screaming. "I love you—why can't you see I love you? I've always loved you, all this time, but you never see! You can't—you don't care. You've never even seen me—who I am. I never want to see you again!" The words tumbled out, far past their time, and I lapsed back into tears.

After a while, I realized my head was buried in his chest. I wondered how long it had been there or if he'd heard anything I said. I looked up at him. His face had caved in, wrecked, as his voice choked out a plea. "Judy, please don't. I can't stand to see you like this."

"I loved you all this time."

His eyes had filled with tears and sorrow. "I'm going to keep crying, too. Please . . . can't you stop? I can't stand to see you cry like this."

To my ears, Jim's voice had taken a paternal tone, telling me how to behave. I stopped crying and coolly appraised the person I'd endowed with holy qualities.

"I'm sorry," he said. "I know I've been unfeeling."

For a moment, and forever, I reached over to understand him. The part of him that wounded others was the weakness that destroyed him even more. His own pain made him blind to how he affected others. Self-obsession drove him—he couldn't drive himself. It was as if he held a sharp blade turned inward as he pushed out against the world. That only pushed the knife farther in, embedding in his heart as he struck out, each time drawing more blood.

"How old are you now?" he asked suddenly. Bristling at the irrelevance, I didn't answer his question.

"Twenty-four?"

I stared at him and shook my head.

"Twenty-three?"

I shook my head again, feeling the anger grow. He sounded incredulous, though he'd known my age for years.

"Twenty-two?"

"No," I said.

"Twenty-one?"

I finally nodded. I was only twenty-one: a child, a baby, green. That was why I couldn't handle things. Just give me a few years, and all these lies would be an everlasting bouquet of roses. My age was the problem . . . but that could improve with time.

Smiling feebly, I got up, smoothed down my hair and clothes for good, and walked to the door, speechless. Following after me, Jim took my hand. He didn't want me bitter.

"I promise I'll call as soon as John's wedding's over, probably late in the afternoon. We can go to the movies. All right?" He acted as if we could restore the romance.

"Uhm-hmn." I nodded, looking at the naked man in the door.

"You look like a pioneer woman." He smiled.

"Yeah. I'll see you," I said.

He kissed me good-bye, and the door shut. Final.

Comin' Back to Me

It was muggy and hot when I got home from the Hyatt House. The air was thick with grime, cars coated with small chunks of ash. Sitting on the cold cement doorstep, I watched the sprinklers wet the grass and caught a whiff of Jim's skin on my fingers. The smell of his sweat was sharp, bitter. It reminded me of too much alcohol, and sour, toxic exhaustion. I didn't wash it off. Janis Joplin had just died, which seemed ominous in a way I couldn't quite comprehend.

The next day, CalArts started: my junior year of art school. I wore a dark-blue midi skirt with a flared bottom, a silky, tight lavender top, and a necklace of black shells. I scoped out the guys and was pleased to see Jack, an old lover who was now a TA. Some of the teachers looked good, too. Soon I was doing installations with cheesecloth, burning ropes over dirt hills, and photographing eggs in holes. I arranged silk over bricks and hung feathers on fiber-filled totems. The school was giddy with excitement, giving us separate studio space, sponsoring trips to make and see art in San Francisco. Artists and money came together; life bloomed.

Later that year, I moved to a guesthouse in the Hollywood Hills. It was down a long, dirt lane lined with trees and the foothill's rambling green. I liked the earth crunching under my car wheels, the huge sunflowers peeking past the calico curtains into my window. At night, with my antique lamps turned off, the city stretched below, like multicolored jewels softly beckoning. This was a sanctuary, my first place of peace. I retreated gratefully into the quiet, wrote poems and baked banana bread, a secret hippie on the hill after spending each day making art. I saw different men and tried not to think about Jim. I could place him in the past or future but couldn't imagine him in my present, though I secretly held out hope for later.

At a certain point, I stopped listening to Doors music because it upset me. Though I heard stories, I didn't want to know what he was doing. I first heard "L.A. Woman" at a friend of a friend's who had slept with him. She thought she was the one. But when I heard the lines, "If they say I never loved you / You know they are a liar," I cried because it sounded like an apology, particularly the ironic "they."

Winter had taken its fluid California turn toward spring when I heard he'd gone to Paris. Rock obviously hadn't worn well, and he wanted to write, lose his sex symbol image, be taken seriously. The murmured rumors sounded like doctors speculating he had a fifty-fifty chance. Weighing with scales of doubt and hope, I thought he'd eventually put the pieces back together. When he returned in September, I'd ask him for an elaborate apology for having wasted so much of my youth. Until then, I could wait.

When the phone rang at three o'clock one morning in July 1971, I thought it must be Jim, back early. I let the phone ring long enough to gather the composure I was surprised to lose so easily. The old symptoms returned: wildly beating heart, difficulty swallowing, breathlessness. I felt disappointed in myself, really, after all these months. "Hello?"

Over the static of long-distance wires, I heard Greg, Kathy's old boyfriend. "Where are you?" I asked. "The phone sounds weird."

"I'm in New York. It's hot. Have you heard about Jim?" he asked.

My mind went blank and swam, dizzy and sick. There was only one thing to hear about Jim. I'd heard everything else a thousand times before. Silence echoed.

"He's dead . . ." I said, my words not a question, but a muffled, terror-stricken pronouncement. I waited to be contradicted. But the pause lasted too long. Greg could hang up now, message delivered.

"Yes," he said.

"Greg, you're drunk. You're drunk, aren't you?"

"Yeah. I've been drunk ever since I found out. It's already hot here. I feel terrible. I kept thinking someone should tell you, before you woke up to the media. I felt close to him, you know . . ." He trailed off incoherently while my body oozed out of itself, an overturned catsup bottle.

"This is a bad joke. It's not a very funny way to test my reactions. You know I'm not over him."

"Judy, it's true. It's true. There's even some story about how he and a friend were walking around the Père Lachaise Cemetery, just a few days before, talking about a nice place to be buried. Something about him picking a plot for himself. Like he knew . . . I think he knew."

"That's sick!"

"I don't know if it's true. It's just a story," he said.

"Is Jim dead or not?" I asked.

"Jim's dead. What do you think I'm calling for?"

"I don't see how. What did he die from—how could he die?"

"Natural causes."

"Natural causes!" That was totally unbelievable, even for Jim.

"Something about a blood clot in his heart," Greg said.

"I don't believe it! But if you're not careful, the same thing will happen to you. You'd better stop drinking—I'm not kidding. You drink too much and you think it's poetic and see what it does. It kills you! He's probably making a documentary on his death."

"He's dead." Greg was stubborn, another poet who wanted to be a filmmaker.

"If you don't stop drinking, you're gonna kill yourself, you know. The same thing—it's gonna happen," I warned.

"I know. That's why I'm drunk."

"I don't believe this. Just a minute." I held the phone away, covered it, and concentrated on the air. I couldn't feel that Jim's energy was gone. The essence of the atmosphere hadn't changed. "Greg? I don't think he's dead. I don't sense a loss of his presence. I can't feel it. At least he's not dead in California."

"Are you all right?" Greg asked. "He really is dead, believe me, I . . . ."

"Yeah, I'm all right. You just better stop drinking!"

"Do you want me to call you back in a little while? To see if you're OK?"

"I'm OK. I don't want to believe it, and I don't want to talk, either."

"I'll call you back later."

"Yeah. Thanks. Good-bye." I hung up the phone and stared at my bedspread. Brown crushed velvet mountains and valleys. I would go down in there, I would . . .

I picked up the phone and dialed KFWB, an all-night news station. An official, hectic-sounding man answered.

"Is Jim Morrison dead?" I asked, waiting for him to laugh. He didn't.

"Yes. Jim Morrison died in Paris, Saturday." He minced no words.

"Oh," I said. "Thanks." I hung up.

Something beyond disbelief convulsed inside me, flung my body up and down. Tears broke into screams muffled by the pillow, coming out, "No, no, no," until even "no" died away. The black sky changed to a gray dawn, but the moon was still there, hanging above the tree branches. Betraying moon, spinning globe, stop the breath in me. He'd let the life slip out of him; it seemed like his final rejection of this world. I felt trapped in my body, captive in the punishing container. I wanted out, too. I got out of bed, walked to my front porch and sat, watching the day rise. I studied the wrists God dared make beautiful, white, and bare. But I couldn't touch them; I had to live. My wrists remained beautiful, white, unmarked. Three years would pass before I could register what had happened.

The End

After Janis and Jimi died, after the trial, after Jim claimed he'd be "number three," he only confirmed what everyone else wouldn't say—at least in front of him. When I look at photos of Jim and Pam in Paris, under their thin smiles I see a terrible deadness in his eyes and barely suppressed anger and shame in hers. They seem to be reluctantly hurtling toward a destruction neither has the power left to stop. Sometimes even the inevitable seems surprising. After secretly rehearsing for the end, it finally happened. It still hurts. It's still death. It's forever. But at the time, it seemed harder to die on purpose than OD by miscalculation. I cut off all my hair and stopped wearing makeup. I joined the Feminist Art Program at CalArts. Then I graduated, went to grad school, and, as if to contradict myself, worked as a model. It was, after all, the 1970s.

Even before we met, it seemed like I was waiting for time to catch up with Jim and me. When he'd told me, "We have plenty of time," it made perfect sense. We were young, I was in art school, he was caught up in being a rock star, and Pam was his main girlfriend—but eventually that would change. I could give it a few more years on the back burner; he'd slow down, they'd break up, and he'd finally realize I was the one. However, once they were both dead, this seemed harder to believe. I finally went to Paris in 1974.

My face ached to maintain anonymous dignity as the Paris Métro approached the cemetery. The people surging around me couldn't have possibly known why I was there, but I thought they might. Getting off at the Père Lachaise station, I imagined spies watching me. That woman selling magazines and candy as I walked up the stairs, that man in the shoe repair shop, shadowy figures lurking in the alleys: they could be taking notes. "Sunday, 2 PM. Female, early twenties, print scarf covering wisps of reddish hair, loose flowing blouse and jeans. If not American, then Nordic, tall and thin, high cheekbones. Appears nervous, suspicious, and very serious." I wondered, Would he recognize my description? Would he recognize me walking here?

Then an old, mumbling French guy was distracting me. Whether he was talking about his cigarette, cigarettes in general, or perhaps just asking for a match, I didn't know. Despite my vehemently repeating "No," he waved his unlit cigarette through the air and chased me to the cemetery entrance. I scrambled up the steps knowing the maniac had totally ruined my lady-in-mourning image. Reaching the top, I turned, majestically cold, to glare in indignation. His mumbling still didn't stop. However, a cemetery guard spotted us and came over, looking angry. The two men exchanged a few gruff words, and the cigarette pervert retreated, shamefaced, down the stairs.

His rescue complete, the guard began his routine. Babbling with emphatic gestures, he determined I was

American, a tourist. Didn't I need a map? It would help me find whom I was looking for. The map flashed as he named famous dead people in wide mystic circles. Sarah Bernhardt, Edith Piaf, Colette, and Chopin were here. Oscar Wilde, Marcel Proust? I gave up and scrawled "Morrison." Ah, he nodded. Yes, yes, of course. . . . Grinning, he drew lines across the map, forming a significant rectangle and a triumphant X to mark the spot. Reveling in the return of chivalry, I thanked him, only to be asked for money. I threw out a few francs and fled.

The map felt almost decadent but, worse, nearly indecipherable. Jim was in section 6 of the miniature town of cobblestoned alleys leading up and around the ancient, forbidding houses of the dead. Like monks' cells or tiny pyramids, rusty and rain-eaten, they jutted in stiff, jagged lines to the sky. There were more modern versions: shiny black marble slabs with sparkly silver flakes and ivory flowers, never to wilt. I desperately hoped he wasn't in one of those.

Finally reaching a major intersection, I turned and noticed the guard balancing on one foot, leaning over to watch me. Yes, I thought, I'm dangerous, another potential grave robber. Only recently I'd asked why they didn't just dig up the damn grave and see what was down there. I moved away from the guard's scrutiny. Hiding behind a tree, breathing in slowly, I consulted my rumpled map and realized I was smack-dab in the middle of section 5E. Piercing French nearly cracked the air, making the cemetery feel bizarrely foreign. Three white-haired women hunched, shrieking over a gravestone. I waited for them to leave, imagining I was a detached historian of the sixties.

I finally entered Jim's section. It was a graffiti environment, maybe four by five mausoleums thick, crammed with multilingual phrases, epitaphs, and revelations. I read out-pourings saluting the embodiment of our universal spirit, flung neat, compact, and complete into one dead body—followed, worshipped, and chased to the grave. "Jim was not a junkie," "No hope without dope," "Have a good trip in Père Lachaise," "You are immortal," "Fuck me," "My only love," "Meet me at desert shore," "Will you give me sanctuary," "Wait for me," "I came back for you," "We all loved you," "Get high forever," "I'll never forget you," "You were beautiful," "You are beyond death."

Circling round the grave, I sniffed the air, alarmed and offended by the graffiti. Throwing my head back, I shook it in refusal, a "no" on my lips. I circled more cautiously, an animal skirting the edges of safety. Revulsion transformed to pain as I glared in anger at the scrawled words and then back down to what sacred thing had been desecrated. Falling against the other tombs, I scraped my body close and hard against them, as if to erase and smooth the words away. I bent over, scanning the full, unmarked view of his grave. It was like a miniature swimming pool filled with yellow and white flowers. My vision focused. I could see the tiny black bugs crawling in the dirt. I stared at them intently, my body stiffening, my face frozen as I wiped my eyes. Tiny bugs in black earth—that was the real end, not just his death. Tears spilled over and over, stopping only to start again, betraying something I wished not to believe.

I made the sign of the cross over my heart. Though I'd come from no real religion, I'd always felt better when I made that gesture, especially after seeing run-over cats, dogs, or deer. And I was thinking, God bless you if you're dead, Jim. God bless you. I looked at that mess of a death, all the need and greed and want still surrounding him, saying it was love, love, love, still saying it's love. I heard approaching voices and wanted to leave before the bells got any closer. A guy and two maroon-haired girls with black fingernails approached; one cried "Jim Morrison," using a soft *j* in that Parisian way. They pounced forward in hungry authority as I slipped away, unnoticed. I gave one backward glance, anguished and angry, partly for Jim, partly for me, but mostly for no one, nothing.

I walked down another cobblestone alley to the cemetery's main street. Leaving felt clean and clear; the trees cast a deep, comforting shade. But I wasn't looking up, something plunged me down into the brownish-black stone depths, and the wet earth felt cool and mossy, rushing up to me in rich, muted tones. A blur of emotion stung my eyes, tears made softer with the repetitive chant: We all die, we all die, we all die. I was back on a street in the outside world, passing a flower shop as I walked to the Métro, thinking I should've brought flowers, thinking I'm glad I didn't. We all die, we all die, we all die.

Dreams

My last morning in the hospital, I saw Jim floating at the foot of my bed. His face was radiant, surrounded by a silver-blue aura. The aqua glowed, reverberated like low humming. I looked up, and his eyes were the world. Simultaneously blue, green, and brown, flecked with knowledge of everything. His eyes were dead, and they were alive—gazing steadily through time into mine. "You'll always love me," he said. "I love you." His voice was audible as bells, gently ringing. "I forgive you," he said. Shimmering, he dissolved back into the bluish transparency of dawn. Almost like he was God.

It was odd, but I felt deeply comforted, relieved and blessed to be forgiven. For the last time, I believed he was God, finally acknowledging me . . . and I felt loved, despite my flaws. For being superficial when I thought I was deep, dependent when I thought I was free. For being proud, needy, and selfish. For years of delusion. He wasn't a god, not even close, but I could forgive him, too. For treating me as if I existed only when he was present, for a self-absorbed view of the universe. And I could forgive myself for the same thing, never truly knowing him.

That last night in the hospital, I saw Jim's body stretched out naked on a slab of stone, yards beneath me. I spiraled down, circled round, and then dove closer, an eagle over its prey. Reaching the ground, I stalked the boundaries of his open grave. I walked around and around, analyzing the body. He had the same skin—the fine, white translucency, a softness in his pores. He had the same delicate molding—the fine precision of his hip bones, a slight, gentle contour to his stomach. He had the same hair—near black, lustrous, lush against the white skin. The same detached, classic beauty had finally attained inhuman perfection. It was cold, hollow art. He was dead. . . . And I flew away, vanishing to a speck on the horizon.